OPTIMIST RACING
OP 级帆船竞赛

A manual for sailors, parents & coaches

Steve Irish & Phil Slater

[英] 史蒂夫·爱尔兰　　[英] 菲尔·斯莱特　著

杨　玉　译

黑版贸登字08-2023-062号

图书在版编目（CIP）数据

OP级帆船竞赛/（英）史蒂夫·爱尔兰
（Steve Irish），（英）菲尔·斯莱特（Phil Slater）
著；杨玉译. -- 哈尔滨：哈尔滨工业大学出版社，
2024. 8.-- ISBN 978-7-5767-1631-3

Ⅰ. G861.419

中国国家版本馆CIP数据核字第2024QX9086号

All Rights Reserved. Authorised translation from the English language edition published by FernhurstBooks Limited. Responsibility for the accuracy of the translation rests solely with Vanhang Sailing and is not the responsibility of Fernhurst Books Limited. No part of this book may be reproduced in any form without the written permission of the original copyright holder.

策划编辑	薛　力
责任编辑	陈　洁
装帧设计	博鑫设计
出版发行	哈尔滨工业大学出版社
社　　址	哈尔滨市南岗区复华四道街10号　邮编150006
传　　真	0451-86414749
网　　址	http://hitpress.hit.edu.cn
印　　刷	哈尔滨市石桥印务有限公司
开　　本	787 mm×1 092 mm　1/16　印张10.5　字数332千字
版　　次	2024年8月第1版　2024年8月第1次印刷
书　　号	ISBN 978-7-5767-1631-3
定　　价	138.00元

（如因印装质量问题影响阅读，我社负责调换）

序

十几年前，当我还在从事足球工作的时候，在一次和英超代表的交流中，曾毫不掩饰地表达过对英国足球的羡慕，有人问我：羡慕他们什么呢？是他们曾经获得过世界杯冠军？是他们曾经培养过杰克·查尔顿、大卫·贝克汉姆、韦恩·鲁尼这样的世界级足球明星？还是他们每场6万的现场球迷？我说：这些都是。但最重要的，是羡慕他们把上述所有这些和更多没有提到的都叠加在一起——他们拥有一个完整、现代并不断完善的足球治理体系——培训体系、青训体系、竞赛体系、理论体系、宣传体系、市场体系！正是因为有了这样一个强大的体系，才使得英格兰足球在经历低谷后还能迅速回归和攀升，并持续走在世界前列！

足球如此，英国帆船难道不更是这样吗？从2000年以来的6届奥运会，他们获得的奖牌总数达到29块（15金、10银、4铜），平均每届获得近5块奖牌，其中平均每届获得2.5块金牌。这靠的又是什么？同样靠的是治理体系……这里面包含着他们几十年、几代人的不懈努力和积累！

理论体系是英国保持领先的重要法宝之一。英国皇家帆船协会有着近百种教学课程，并拥有理论分析和教学的书籍近千本。我们今天看到的这本《OP级帆船竞赛》可能只是英国浩瀚帆船理论中的一滴水，但仅仅这一滴水也让我们深受感悟！

这本书，让我们重新审视了现代帆船运动的基础——OP帆船，对帆船普及和帆船竞技的重要作用。无论是作为世界上保有量最大的帆船类别，还是对于站上世界比赛、奥运比赛、职业大帆船比赛最高领奖台的那些冠军们，OP帆船无疑功不可没。小小OP，不容小视，它是打开孩子们对帆船最初认识和喜爱的一扇窗，更是孩子们不断积累技术、知识、经验，走向更大船型、更高竞赛舞台的一条大路！

这本书，让我们再次认识到现代竞技体育已经远远不是仅仅凭借着天赋就可以获得优异成绩，帆船竞赛更是如此，它是技术、体能、智慧、知识、心理、战术等一系列综合能力的较量。这本书用简洁生动的语言告诉孩子们应该如何努力才能进步，才能获胜！

这本书，不仅仅为那些参与OP竞赛的孩子们提供一本有益的训练指南，也是小帆船教练们强化理论并结合实际探讨如何更好施教的教学提纲，甚至是劝导家长如何更好陪伴自己的孩子走好帆船道路的指导。不同的读者站在不同的角度去学习和领会，并根据自身的情况去实践，相信大家一定会各得其所，必有受益！

感谢本书的作者，把他和同伴们有益的经验汇集成理论分享给我们！感谢万航帆艇，在我们理论建设尚处于初级阶段的时候，开始着手开展这项基础工作，难能可贵！

为了孩子们，为了未来，我们需要学习，更需要和欢迎更多从业者参与中国帆船的理论建设。

孩子们，加油！同行们，加油！中国帆船，加油！

刘卫东
2024年5月10日

FOREWORD 前　言

I will never forget my years in the Optimist class. My family didn't have a background in sailing and so, with endless support from my parents, it was the dedicated coaches in Wales who got my sailing career started. Just as Phil and Jill Slater did for Ben Ainslie.

我永远不会忘记我驾驶OP的岁月。我的家族没有航海背景，因此，在我父母无尽的支持下，是威尔士专业的教练们开启了我的航海生涯。就像菲尔（Phil）和吉尔·斯莱特（Jill Slater）为本·安斯利（Ben Ainslie）所做的那样。

The competition, the camaraderie and the fun of sailing an Optimist helped develop my love of sailing and with it the results started coming, culminating in being the first girl to win the UK Optimist National Championships and the first Brit to win the Optimist Girls' World Championships. Very proud moments for any Optimist sailor!

比赛、友谊以及驾驶OP的乐趣培养了我对帆船的热爱，然后开始取得一些成绩，最终成为第一个获得英国OP全国锦标赛冠军的女孩和第一个获得OP女子世界锦标赛冠军的英国人。对于任何OP水手来说，这都是非常自豪的时刻！

I then moved on to double-handed sailing, first in the 420 and then the 470. I won the World Championship in both, with Steve Irish coaching me to the 420 World Championship title. At the start of my time in the 470, I was also lucky enough to be coached by Steve. He is a fantastic coach, who is patient, knowledgeable and passionate about what he does.

然后，我转向了双人艇，先是420级，然后是470级。我在这两个级别都获得了世界冠军，史蒂夫·爱尔兰（Steve Irish）指导我获得了420级世界冠军的头衔。在我进入470级别的初期，我也很幸运地得到了史蒂夫（Steve）的指导。他是一位非常出色的教练，对自己的工作充满耐心、博学多才且饱含激情。

Good coaching is fundamental to success in the Optimist class and it is brilliant that Steve has been able to work with Phil updating the original Optimist Racing book, which I remember from my time in the class.

良好的教学是OP级别成功的基础，史蒂夫能够与菲尔一起更新《OP竞赛》的原著，这是非常棒的，我记得上学时就读过这本书。

This book will show you how to sail an Optimist fast. It will teach you about techniques and tuning, boat handling and tactics—it will also offer you a lot of guidance on the physical and mental side of being a great Optimist sailor. I would highly recommend it to any Optimist sailor, no matter what level you are at in your sailing career.

这本书将向你展示如何快速驾驶OP。它将教你相关技巧和调节、船只操控和战术——它还将为你提供很多关于成为一名伟大的OP水手的身心方面的指导。我向每一位OP水手强烈推荐这本书，无论你在航海生涯中处于什么水平。

Good luck in everything you want to achieve, enjoy the racing, push yourself when you are out of your comfort zone, but most importantly have fun! I hope that you really enjoy your Optimist racing and it is just the start of a really successful lifetime of sailing.

祝你一切顺利，期望你能享受比赛，走出舒适区并推自己一把，最重要的是要开心！我希望你真的喜欢 OP 竞赛，这只是一个成功的航海生涯的开始。

Hannah Mills, MBE
Olympic gold & silver medallist (470), World Champion (470, 420, Optimist), UK National Champion (Optimist)

汉娜·米尔斯，MBE
奥运会金牌和银牌得主（470）、世界冠军（470、420、OP）、英国全国冠军（OP）

THE AUTHORS 作　者

INSPIRATIONAL COACHES & SAILORS 鼓舞人心的教练和水手

Steve Irish is a world-class professional sailing coach. He has worked for the British Sailing Team, Turkish Sailing Federation and Thailand's 49er team. This has included coaching a variety of youth and junior squads, enabling 470 sailors to progress from development to Olympic-level funding—including Hannah Mills and Luke Patience—and leading 29er and 420 sailors to international success at championships such as the Youth Sailing Worlds. He coaches Optimist sailors regularly both in the UK and around the world.

史蒂夫·爱尔兰是世界级的职业帆船教练。他曾为英国帆船队、土耳其帆船联合会和泰国49er队效力。这包括指导各种青年队和少年队，使470名水手从创立发展到奥运会级别，包括汉娜·米尔斯（Hannah Mills）和卢克·佩恩斯（Luke Patience），并带领29er级和420级水手在诸如世界青年帆船锦标赛等国际赛事上取得成功。他经常在英国和世界各地指导OP水手。

He is the coach of choice among the UK national champions entering the Endeavour Trophy (the UK's Champion of Champions event) each year.

他是每年参加奋进杯（英国冠军赛）的全国冠军们的首选教练。

Steve's own sailing has encompassed a whole range of classes from junior and youth sailing to Olympic double-handers and high-performance skiffs. As a top Optimist sailor, Steve represented GBR internationally. He went on to become a 420 world champion and then crewed 470s, finishing 5th at the Europeans. He also sailed 49ers and Tornados internationally and subsequently competed in the twin-trapeze RS800 class, winning the national title two years running, while also claiming a podium finish at a 100+ boat RS200 nationals.

史蒂夫自己的帆船生涯涵盖了从少年和青少年帆船到奥运会双人帆船和高性能帆船的所有级别。作为一名顶级OP水手，史蒂夫在国际上代表着英国。他后来成为420级别的世界冠军，继而在470级别中作为缭手，获得欧锦赛第5名的成绩。他还驾驶49er和Tornados级帆船，随后参加了双人吊裤RS800级比赛，在该项目上连续2年获得全国冠军，同时在有100多艘RS200级帆船参赛的赛事上登上领奖台。

Phil Slater was a successful sailor having captained the University of London Sailing Team and won the Firefly National Championships. A doctor in Falmouth, he has been described as a 'local sailing legend' by Ben Ainslie.

菲尔·斯莱特（Phil Slater）是一名成功的水手，曾担任伦敦大学帆船队队长，并赢得了萤火虫（Firefly）级帆船全国锦标赛。作为法尔茅斯的一名医生，他被本·安斯利（Ben Ainslie）称为"当地的航海传奇"。

Phil and his wife Jill set up a programme to encourage the local children into sailing in Optimists at Restronguet Sailing Club. Part of this group was a young Ben Ainslie, who Jill taught to sail and then rapidly progressed into the top group, run by Phil. Soon the group was one of the top Optimist fleets in the country and Phil became an RYA Optimist Racing Coach. He was the UK Optimist Team Coach at numerous championships.

菲尔（Phil）和他的妻子吉尔(Jill)在Restronguet帆船俱乐部设立了一个项目，鼓励当地的孩子们参加OP帆船的学习。这个小组中的一个人就是年轻时的本·安斯利（Ben Ainslie），吉尔（Jill）教授他航海，他随后迅速进入顶级队伍，由菲尔（Phil）管理。很快，这个小组成为美国顶级OP赛队之一，菲尔（Phil）成为英国皇家游艇协会OP竞赛教练。他曾在众多锦标赛中担任英国OP队教练。

He was Ben Ainslie's first sailing coach, training him to win the UK Optimist National Championships and compete in 4 Optimist World Championships. This was the start and foundation for Ben Ainslie's amazing sailing career, including winning 4 Olympic gold medals, multiple world championships and the America's Cup as tactician.

他是本·安斯利（Ben Ainslie）的第一位帆船教练，训练本赢得英国OP全国锦标赛，并参加4届OP世界锦标赛。这是本·安斯利（Ben Ainslie）令人惊叹的帆船生涯的开始和基础，包括赢得4枚奥运金牌、多个世界冠军以及成为美洲杯的战术师。

Phil still races his Firefly with Jill as well as racing a Falmouth working boat and cruising with friends around Europe.

菲尔（Phil）仍然与吉尔（Jill）一起驾驶他的萤火虫（Firefly）级帆船和法尔茅斯级帆船进行比赛，与朋友们在欧洲各地巡游。

INTRODUCTION 简　介

Some people look on the Optimist as a bit of a joke. It's a curvy box that kids learn to sail in! But it is numerically the biggest sailing class in the world, and ex-Optimist sailors have won many gold medals in all the dinghy classes at the Olympics. The boat is, in fact, a remarkable design—an easily-controlled thoroughbred racing dinghy that provides superb one-design racing and responds to and rewards the highest skills of top sailors.

有些人把 OP 看作是一个笑话。这是个有弧度的盒子，孩子们在里面学习帆船！但从数字上看，它是世界上最大的帆船级别，前 OP 水手在奥运会的所有稳向板船级别都获得了许多金牌。事实上，这艘船的设计非凡，是一种易于控制的一流的竞赛帆船，它提供了卓越的统一级别赛事，并响应和奖励最高技能的顶级水手。

The Optimist is sailed by more than 170,000 young people in over 110 countries. Fantastic events take place all around the world, with racing of the highest standard and great fun ashore. Each year there are open meetings, national championships, area championships and a world championship for as many as 259 sailors from 65 countries.

OP 由 110 多个国家的 17 万多名年轻人驾驶。世界各地都有精彩的赛事，这些赛事拥有最高标准和岸上的巨大乐趣。每年有来自大约 65 个国家的 259 名水手参加公开赛、全国锦标赛、地区锦标赛和世界锦标赛。

International Optimist racing is an adventure! It offers the chance of making lasting friendships with top sailors from other countries and representing your country in major international competitions. This book will get you into the action. Its aims are:

国际 OP 竞赛是一场探险！它提供了与来自其他国家的顶级水手建立持久友谊的机会，以及代表你的国家参加重大国际比赛的机会。这本书会让你着手行动。其目标是：

- To help competent Optimist sailors develop handling techniques and boats peed. They should be able to analyse performance, coach themselves, and develop a positive psychological attitude to the stresses of competition to get to the top in national and international racing.
- 帮助有能力的 OP 水手提高控船技术和船速。他们应该能够分析比赛表现，进行自我指导，并对比赛的压力形成积极的心理态度，从而在国内和国际比赛中名列前茅。
- To help parents analyse their own motives for supporting their children's sailing, and to avoid actions that might have a negative effect on their performance and happiness.
- 帮助父母分析自己支持孩子们航海的动机，避免可能对孩子们的表现和幸福产生负面影响的行为。
- To help coaches develop competitor / parent / coach relationships, to understand the constraints of children's development, and to develop race training programmes and techniques.
- 帮助教练建立与竞争对手 / 家长 / 教练的关系，了解儿童发展的制约因素，并制订比赛训练计划和技巧。

Performance depends on physical fitness, mental fitness, boatspeed techniques, boat handling skills, theoretical knowledge, rules knowledge, racing experience, good equipment, parental support and good coaching. Read on to find out how to achieve all these goals.

表现取决于身体素质、心理素质、船速技术、控船技巧、理论知识、规则知识、比赛经验、良好的设备、父母的支持和良好的指导。继续阅读,了解如何实现所有这些目标。

Steve Irish & Phil Slater 史蒂夫·爱尔兰和菲尔·斯莱特

CONTENTS 目 录

PART 1　　SPEED　　　　　　　　　　　　　　　　1
第一部分　速　度

CHAPTER 1　Speed Basics　　　　　　　　　　　2
第一章　基本速度理论

CHAPTER 2　　Sail & Rig　　　　　　　　　　　9
第二章　帆和索具

CHAPTER 3　　Upwind Speed　　　　　　　　　22
第三章　迎风船速

CHAPTER 4　　Downwind Speed　　　　　　　　36
第四章　顺风船速

PART 2　　BOAT HANDLING & TACTICS　　　　49
第二部分　操控与技术

CHAPTER 5　　Basic Boat Handing　　　　　　　50
第五章　基本控船

CHAPTER 6　　Tactics　　　　　　　　　　　　65
第六章　战　术

PART 3　　EQUIPMENT & TUNING　　　　　　77
第三部分　装备 & 调试

CHAPTER 7　　Mast Rake　　　　　　　　　　　78
第七章　桅杆倾度

CHAPTER 8　　Fast Gear　　　　　　　　　　　80
第八章　速航装备

| PART 4 | WIND & CURRENT | 91 |

第四部分　风 & 流

| CHAPTER 9 | Seeing The Wind | 92 |

第九章　看　风

| CHAPTER 10 | Understanding Current | 100 |

第十章　理解涌流

| PART 5 | MIND & BODY | 107 |

第五部分　精神 & 身体

| CHAPTER 11 | Mental Fitness | 108 |

第十一章　心理健康

| CHAPTER 12 | The Perfect Body | 114 |

第十二章　完美体格

| CHAPTER 13 | Physical Fitness | 117 |

第十三章　体　能

| PART 6 | PARENTS & COACHES | 129 |

第六部分　父母 & 教练

| CHAPTER 14 | For Parents | 130 |

第十四章　写给父母

| CHAPTER 15 | The Perfect Coach | 135 |

第十五章　完美教练

SPEED
速 度

PART 1 第一部分

CHAPTER 1 第一章
Speed Basics 基本速度理论

Sailing fast is the aim of all top sailors! It's great to leave the start line and feel the boat drawing ahead, looking back and knowing you have the speed and the other boats are not going to catch you. But how do you gain such speed?

快速航行是所有顶级水手的目标！离开起航线时，你遥遥领先，当你回头看时，你知道自己保持很好的速度，并且其他船只都追不上你，这种感觉真是太棒了。但是，你要怎样才能有这样的速度呢？

Some people seem to sail fast naturally, while others never get a top ten result. The single thing that will help you go faster is to spend as much time as possible sailing. Get to know the feel of your boat—how she responds to changes of wind strength and wave state. You will begin to feel when the boat is balanced, when she sails herself with only small movements of the tiller. You will recognise how the balance is changed by trim, mast and daggerboard rake, sail sheeting and, upwind, the relative value of sailing fast and free or pointing higher and going a little slower.

有些人看上去自然而然就能航行得很快，但有些人却从来没有获得过前十的成绩。一件能够帮助你更快航行的事情是你花尽可能多的时间去航行。感受你的船——她如何回应风力和浪的变化。你会开始感受到什么时候船是平衡的，什么时候她只用小幅度动舵来航行。你会意识到，如何通过调整索具、桅杆和稳向板倾斜度、拉帆来保持平衡，以及迎风航行时，是快速自由航行，还是以更小角度航行，但速度稍微慢一些。

Learn the skills of sailing upwind and down in light, medium and heavy weather, in smooth and rough water, on lakes and the open sea. Learn to sit at the boat's pivot point, leaning back, balanced, allowing your upper body to float freely as the boat moves easily through the waves. Learn efficient boat handling, power hiking and bailing. Seek to gain automatic reflex boat control. Allow 'trust' your body to do the sailing while you keep your mind busy monitoring sail trim, tactics, tides, stress, etc. Learn to sail in a state of relaxed concentration, get 'in the groove', 'slip into the fast lane'!

在小风、中风、大风，在平静水面和不平静的水面，在湖里和开放海域，学习迎风和顺风航行技术。学着坐在船的旋转中心上，身体向后倾斜，保持平衡，让你的上半身自由移动，使得船只更容易地穿过浪。学习有效地控船、加力和减力，获得船只操控时的肌肉记忆。当你的大脑忙于调帆、战术、潮汐、处理压力时，要信任你的身体去完成航行。学会在专注轻松的状态下航行，进入"最佳状态"，"进入快速航行的航线"！

Speed! Feel it, live it and spot anything that might damage it.

船速！感受它，体验它，注意任何能够破坏它的因素。

Balance
左右平衡

A boat is in balance when it virtually sails itself with the rudder pointing along the centreline, producing minimal drag. A balanced boat is a fast boat; always seek balance.

处于左右平衡状态的船只，当舵放在船的中

CHAPTER 1 第一章　Speed Basics 基本速度理论

心线上时，它会自己航行，此时产生很小的阻力。平衡的船是快的船，所以要一直寻求船的平衡。

- Weather helm is present when the tiller needs to be pulled to windward to keep the boat sailing in a straight line
- 上风舵出现在需要将舵拉向上风方向来保持船只直线行驶的时候
- Lee helm is present when the tiller needs to be pushed to leeward to keep the boat sailing in a straight line
- 下风舵出现在需要将舵推向下风方向来保持船只直线行驶的时候
- If the rudder is needed to keep the boat on course, it is slowing you down
- 如果需要用舵来保持船只的航线，它正在降低你的船速

However, a little weather helm can help upwind by generating lift and this can outweigh the added drag but be really careful it isn't too much! Aim to have the tiller so it has a slight pull and if you let go of it the boat would slowly head up. It shouldn't feel like a fight to steer. If your tiller arm is starting to ache after being on the same tack for a while you definitely have too much weather helm!

然而，轻微的上风舵在迎风航行时可以通过抬高角度有所助益，平衡掉额外增加的阻力，但是需要十分小心，不能太多！目标是让主舵柄有轻微的拉力，如果你松开主舵柄，船就会慢慢迎风偏转。这不是与舵的争斗。如果保持一舷航行一段时间之后，拿舵的手开始酸痛，那肯定是上风舵太多了！

Right amount of weather helm
左右平衡航行

COR Versus COE 阻力中心 VS 受力中心

The Centre of Resistance (COR) is the point under the boat where the combined force of water pressure on the hull and foils (daggerboard and rudder) resisting sideslip or 'leeway' is centred. It is typically slightly behind the daggerboard.

阻力中心指的是在船下的，船体和防止船只横移的块状部件（稳向板和舵）上的水压的合力点。它通常在稳向板的后侧一点点。

The Centre of Effort (COE) is the point in the sail where all the sideways forces are centred.

受力中心是帆上所有侧倾力的合力点。

- If the COE is aligned with the COR, the boat

Too much weather helm
太多上风舵

Too much lee helm
太多下风舵

Balanced helm
左右平衡航行

OPTIMIST RACING OP 级帆船竞赛

is balanced.
- 如果受力中心和阻力中心在一条线上，则船是平衡的。
- If the COE is forward of the COR, the boat's bow will bear off from the wind. This gives 'lee helm'.
- 如果受力中心在阻力中心的前侧，船头会顺风偏转远离风，这就是"下风舵"。
- If the COE is behind the COR, the boat's bow will turn up into the wind. This gives 'weather helm'.
- 如果受力中心在阻力中心的后侧，船头会迎风偏转靠近风，这就是"上风舵"。

Mast Rake 桅杆倾斜度

Rake is important in the search for a balanced boat. If the mast is raked back, the sail's COE acts behind the COR, and turns the boat into the wind. If the mast is raked forward, the sail's COE acts forward of the COR, making the boat bear away.

平衡的船只，桅杆倾斜度是一个重要考量因素。如果桅杆后倾，帆上的受力中心在阻力中心之后，这会让船迎风偏转。如果桅杆前倾，帆上的受力中心在阻力中心之前，这会让船顺风偏转。

Daggerboard Angle 稳向板角度

When the daggerboard is fully down you can use the elastic loop (attached to the sides of the daggerboard case) to hold it vertical, raked forward or raked aft. When the daggerboard is raked forward, the COR moves forward. When the board is raked back, the COR moves back. If the boat was in a state of balance with the daggerboard vertical, raking it forward would give you weather helm and raking it back would give you lee helm.

当稳向板全部放下的时候，你可以用弹力绳（绑在稳向板槽侧边的）保持其垂直、前倾或者后倾。当稳向板前倾，阻力中心前移。当稳向板后倾，阻力中心后移。如果稳向板垂直的时候船处于平衡状态，稳向板前倾可以导致上风舵，稳向板后倾可以造成下风舵。

Centre of Effort in front of Centre of Resistance
受力中心在阻力中心之前

Move helm & dagger-board back. Rake rig forward.
舵手后移及稳向板后倾，帆前倾。

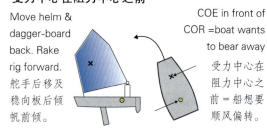

COE in front of COR = boat wants to bear away
受力中心在阻力中心之前 = 船想要顺风偏转

Cetre of Effort behind of Centre of Resistance
受力中心在阻力中心之后

Move helm & daggerboard forward. Rake rig back.
舵手前移及稳向板前倾，帆后倾。

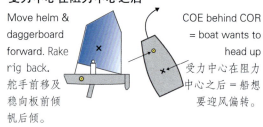

COE behind COR = boat wants to head up
受力中心在阻力中心之后 = 船想要迎风偏转

Cetre of Effort over Centre of Resistance
受力中心在阻力中心之上

Helm in middle & daggerboard straight down.
舵手在中间并且稳向板垂直向下。

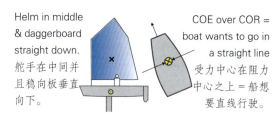

COE over COR = boat wants to go in a straight line
受力中心在阻力中心之上 = 船想要直线行驶

✗ Centre of effort is around the draft (deepest / most powerful point) of the sail. This has some force to leeward as well as driving the boat forward.
受力中心约在帆的最深处（最深或者最有力的点）。这个力会让船往下风横移和向前行驶。

⊙ Centre of resistance is around the helm weight and aft edge of the daggerboard and this opposes the forces driving the boat to leeward.
阻力中心约在舵手的身体重量和稳向板的后侧边缘附近，并与让船往下风横移的力量相反。

⚲ Helm.
舵手

The effect of the Centre of Effort and Centre of Resistance
受力中心和阻力中心的影响

Daggerboard Height 稳向板的高度

In heavy weather you may need to lift the daggerboard to decrease the heeling moment and cut down weather helm. As the underwater portion of the daggerboard decreases, the COR moves up and back towards the rudder.

在强风天气，你可能需要将稳向板抬起一点，以减轻侧倾力和上风舵。稳向板在水下的部分减少时，阻力中心向上和向后至舵的方向移动。

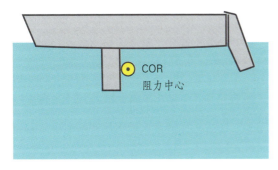

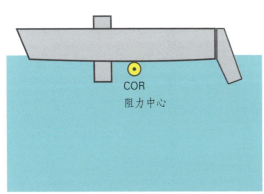

The COR moves up and back when the board is lifted
稳向板抬起，阻力中心向上和向后移动

To keep the boat in balance, the mast can be raked back as the daggerboard is lifted. Lightweights will find it difficult to keep the boat flat in heavy weather, so keep balance by lifting the daggerboard with the mast upright or forward which reduces the weather helm and makes the boat easier to sail.

为保持船的左右平衡，抬起稳向板的时候，可以将桅杆后倾。体重较轻的水手会发现在强风天气很难保持船的左右平衡，因此，通过桅杆直立或向前、抬起稳向板来保持船的左右平衡，将减轻上风舵，并让船更容易航行。

Sheeting The Sail 拉帆

As the sail is sheeted in towards the centreline the COE moves back and makes the boat head up into the wind. This can be used to tack a stationary boat—you simply pull the sail in slowly, and the boat will spin through the wind. Similarly, balance changes when the sail is let out in gusts.

帆逐渐向船的中心线拉紧的时候，受力中心向后移动，船迎风偏转。缓慢拉帆——这个技巧可用来让一条静态的船迎风换舷，船会转向风。类似地，阵风时松帆也可以改变左右平衡。

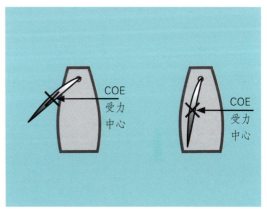

The COE moves back as the sail is pulled in
帆拉紧时受力中心向后移动

Sail Shape 帆形

Due to its cut or the way it is set, sail shape can also considerably affect the balance of a boat. An over-tight leech moves the COE back, while an open leech has the opposite effect. The sprit and kicking strap (vang) are important, because of their effects on the leech.

由于帆的裁剪或设计，帆的形状也会显著影响船的平衡。一面帆后缘过紧的帆会使受力中心后移，一面帆后缘打开的帆则会产生相反的效果。斜撑杆和斜拉器比较重要，因为它们会影响帆后缘。

OPTIMIST RACING OP 级帆船竞赛

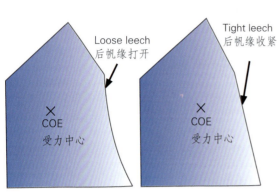

The COE moves back as the leech is tightened
帆后缘收紧时受力中心后移

Heeling (Lateral Trim) 倾斜（横向平衡）

The asymmetric underwater shape and, in particular, the effect of water pressure on the submerged lee bow, causes the boat to turn away from the immersed side. Heel can be used on all legs of the course to balance the boat and sail more quickly. For example, you can heel to windward on the beats to balance weather helm; on the run, heeling to windward balances the rotational force of the mainsail; bearing away around marks is much easier if the boat is heeled to windward.

不对称的水下形状，特别是水压对于水下下风船头的影响，导致船从浸没的一侧转向。倾斜可以用于航线的各个航段，使船平衡和更快速航行。例如，横风航行时，你可以向上风倾斜，来平衡上风舵；顺风航行时，向上风倾斜以平衡主帆上的旋转力；如果船向上风倾斜，顺风偏转绕标将更加容易。

Fore-And-Aft Trim 前后平衡

The two aims in trimming the boat fore-and-aft are to try to prevent the bow from hitting the waves, and to try to prevent the stern dragging too deeply in the water. This is achieved with the boat sailing with its sheer line level. Lightweights will have to sit well back in moderate to fresh winds to prevent the bow from dipping.

让船达到前后平衡，有两个目标，一是防止船头拍浪，二是试着防止船尾过多地拖水。这通过船只直线平衡行驶来实现。在中风到大风时，体重较轻的水手需要往后坐以防止船头拍浪。

Heavyweights have to strike a happy medium, accepting some stern drag while keeping the boat dead flat which allows the bow to lift as high as possible.

体重较重的水手必须达到一个令人满意的均衡状态，接受一些船身阻力，保持船完全平衡，这可以让船头尽可能地抬起。

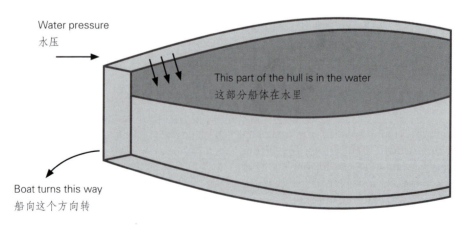

Allowing the boat to heel will make it want to turn
船只倾斜将使其想要转向

CHAPTER 1 第一章　　Speed Basics 基本速度理论

If you sit too far back, the transom drags due to eddies and turbulence
如果你坐得太靠后，水流漩涡和乱流会造成船尾阻力

If you sit too far forward, the bow hits the waves and stops you
如果你坐得太靠前，船头拍浪会让你减速

TOP TIPS 几点建议

- Hold the tiller extension like a dagger, little finger nearest the universal joint.
- 像握匕首一样握副舵柄，小拇指离万向节最近。
- Hold the mainsheet in the same way, little finger nearest the block—thumbs up!
- 用同样的方式抓主帆缭绳，小拇指离滑轮组最近——拇指向上。
- Hike leaning back, knees and feet together, pulling the sheet with your elbow high.
- 压舷时身体往后倾斜，膝盖和双脚并拢，拉帆时手肘抬高。
- Keep the boat and rig balanced, and the rudder on the centreline. Try not to fight the rudder.
- 保持船和帆的平衡，舵放在中心线上。别尝试与舵斗争。
- Don't let the bow hit waves. Bail as soon as any water gets in the boat and sail to keep the boat dry.
- 别让船头拍浪。一旦船内有水，就舀出去，保持船内干燥的状态航行。

PRACTICE IDEAS 训练计划

Steering Without The Rudder 无舵航行

Using the rudder always slows the boat down. You can steer the boat without the rudder, using the following techniques:

用舵会让船速减慢。使用以下技巧，你可以在不用舵的情况下让船转向：

1. A boat with lee helm can be balanced, or a balanced boat may be made to luff (turn into the wind) by:

   以下技巧，可以让处于下风舵状态的船只平衡，或者让平衡的船只迎风偏转（转向风）：

   - Heeling to leeward
   - 向下风倾斜
   - Bringing the COE of the sail aft—by raking the mast back, sheeting in the sail more or tightening the leech
   - 将受力中心后移——通过桅杆后倾、拉帆或者让帆后缘变紧
   - Bringing the COR forward—by raking the daggerboard forward or moving yourself forward
   - 将阻力中心前移——通过稳向板前倾或者人往前移动

2. A boat with weather helm can be balanced, or a balanced boat can be made to bear away (turn away from the wind) by:

   以下技巧，可以让处于上风舵状态的船只平衡，或者可以让平衡的船只顺风偏转（驶离风）：

   - Heeling to windward
   - 向上风倾斜
   - Bringing the COE of the sail forward—by raking the mast forward, easing the sail or opening the leech
   - 将受力中心前移——通过桅杆前倾、松帆或者打开帆后缘
   - Bringing the COR aft—by raking the daggerboard aft or raising it or moving yourself towards the stern
   - 将阻力中心后移——通过稳向板后倾或者抬起部分稳向板，或者人往船尾移动

Lash the tiller in the centre with elastic hooked around the toestraps; then practise the techniques described here.

用弹力绳将舵柄固定在中间压舷带上，然后再练习上述技巧。

Sailing with the tiller lashed
固定舵柄航行

CHAPTER 2 第二章
Sail & Rig 帆和索具

The sail and rig are vital components to boat speed, so it is important that they are clearly understood.

帆和索具对于船速来说是非常重要的组成部分，所以清晰理解它们非常重要。

Sail Shape
帆形

Sail shape is the key to pointing high and sailing fast.

帆形是跑高和快速航行的关键。

Pointing depends on the sail's entry, which is the angle between the front of the sail and a line from luff to leech. If this angle is narrow (A) the entry is said to be flat and the boat will point high without backwinding. If wide (B), the entry is full, and the boat will point poorly.

角度取决于帆的风角，风角指的是帆的前部和帆前缘到帆后缘连线的夹角。如果这个角度很小（A），风角很平，船就能跑高且帆前缘不会飘动。如果角度很大（B），风角饱满，船的角度就会比较糟糕。

The point of maximum depth of a sail is called the 'maximum draft'. The power or drive of a sail depends on the depth and the position of the maximum draft. Generally:

帆的深度最大的点我们称之为"最大深度点"，帆的力量大小和驱动力取决于最大深度点的深度和位置，总的来说：

- Full sails are more powerful than flat ones
- 饱满的帆形比扁平的帆形更有力量
- A sail's power increases as the maximum draft moves forward
- 随着最大深度点向前移动，帆上力量逐步加大

- A well-shaped sail has its maximum draft 40% to 50% of the way back from the luff (C)
- 好的帆形的最大深度点在离帆前缘往后 40%~50% 的位置（C）

In sail setting you are seeking the best compromise between pointing and power.
设置帆形时，我们总在寻求角度和力量的最佳折中方案。

In smooth water the boat is not being slowed by waves and can maintain maximum speed with less power. Thus, pointing ability is most important, so set up with a flat entry, fullness further back and a flatter sail.

在平静水面航行，不会有浪降低船速，可以在力量较小的情况下保持最大的船速。因此，角度走高的能力至关重要，所以我们将帆形设置得更平，帆角较小，帆后部饱满。

In rough water wave impact slows the boat and maximum power is needed to keep the speed up. Set up with the maximum draft forward, a wide entry and a full sail.

在有浪的水面航行，船速受浪的影响有所减慢，我们需要最大的力量来保持速度。我们将帆的最大深度点向前设置，风角较大，帆形饱满。

The maximum draft moves towards the relatively tighter side of the sail:

最大深度点会向帆上相对较紧的一侧移动：

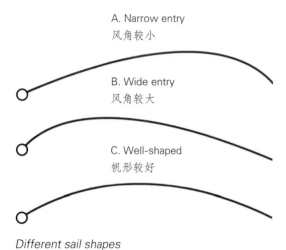

A. Narrow entry
风角较小

B. Wide entry
风角较大

C. Well-shaped
帆形较好

Different sail shapes
不同的帆形

- Forward if the luff is tightened (e.g. if the cunningham is pulled on)
- 帆前缘较紧，最大深度点靠前（例如，下拉器拉紧）
- Aft if the leech is tightened (e.g. if the kicking strap (vang) is applied or mainsheet pulled harder)
- 帆后缘较紧，最大深度点靠后（例如，斜拉器拉紧或者主帆缭绳用力拉紧）
- Down if the foot is tightened (e.g. outhaul pulled in)
- 帆底边较紧，最大深度点靠下（例如，横拉器拉紧）

Sail Drive 帆上的力量

The drive from a sail is due to the pressure difference between the windward and leeward sides. The forces trying to push the boat sideways are cancelled by the force of the water on the daggerboard and rudder foils. With a properly trimmed sail more of the forces are driving forwards.

帆上的力量是由帆的上风侧和下风侧气压差造成的。推动船横移的力量被水作用在稳向板和舵上的力抵消。帆形调整适当时，大部分力量会让船往前走。

Hooked Leech 帆后缘过紧

At no time should your coach, when following straight behind your boat, be able to see the leeward side of your sail. When the leech is hooked in towards the boat's centreline, the driving force from the leech works backwards which is not good!

任何情况下，当你的教练在你的船尾直线跟随的时候，都不应该看到帆的下风侧。当你的帆后缘向船的中心线收紧时，帆后缘的力量就会向后用力，这是不好的！

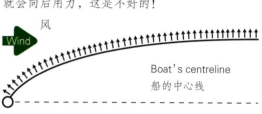

With a correctly trimmed sail—with the leech parallel to the boat's centreline—the boat drives forward
正确设置的帆——帆后缘与船的中心线平行——船向前移动

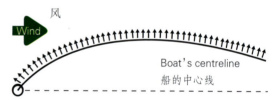

With an incorrectly trimmed sail—which hooks the leech towards the centreline—the driving force from the leech is sideways and backward
错误设置的帆——帆后缘向船的中心线收紧——帆后缘上的力量向下风和后侧

A hooked leech is one of the most common reasons for Optimist sailors going slowly, but how does this come about?

帆后缘过紧是OP水手船速慢的最常见的原因之一，但这是如何发生的呢？

- Excitement and over sheeting
- 过于兴奋，过度拉帆
- Not knowing what a sail looks like when it is 'just right'
- 不知道正确的帆是什么样子
- Too much sprit tension—failure to readjust

the sprit for falling wind strength, so the leech tightens, and the boat stops in the lulls
- 斜撑杆过紧——风力减弱时未能及时调整斜撑杆，导致帆后缘过紧，船在小风区停下
- Variable wind strength—setting the sprit up for the gusts rather than the lulls
- 风力变化——阵风时拉紧斜撑杆，小风区时则相反
- Too much kicking strap (vang) tension—none is required upwind in an Opi, except when spilling wind
- 斜拉器过紧——在OP迎风航行时不需要拉紧，除非需要卸力
- Foot of the sail too slack

- 帆底边太松
- Luff too slack or badly laced
- 帆前缘太松或者没绑好

It helps to look at the top batten. Keep this parallel to the boat's centreline when close hauled. If it angles towards the centre, the leech is hooked. Beware! Leech telltales do not always tell you the leech is hooked.

观察顶部的帆骨会有所帮助。迎风角度时需要确保顶部帆骨与船的中心线平行。如果它向中心线倾斜，帆后缘过紧。请注意！帆后缘的气流线并不总能体现出帆后缘过紧。

A hooked leech—one of the most common reasons for going slowly
帆后缘过紧是船速慢的最常见原因之一

Rig Controls 帆与索具

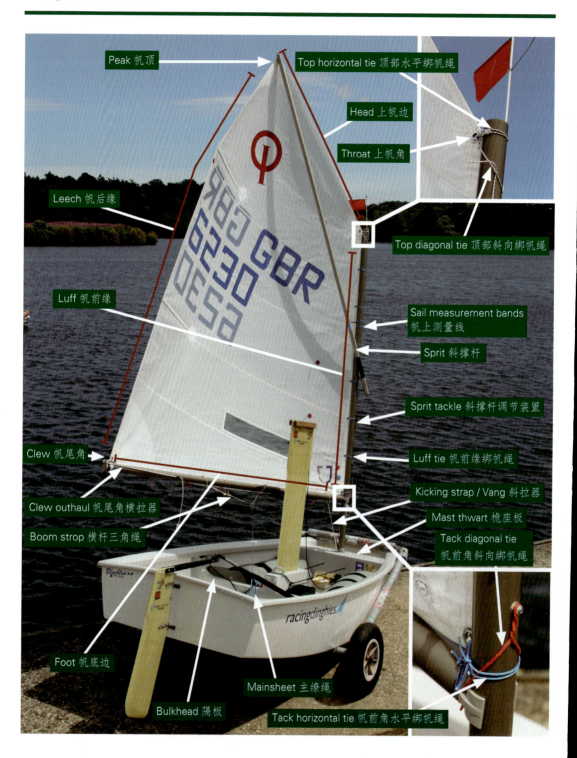

Sprit 斜撑杆

The key to understanding the sprit is to realise that the head of a sail cannot be stretched. Sprit thrust holds up the peak and tensions the leech.

理解斜撑杆的关键是意识到上帆边无法伸展。因此，斜撑杆撑起了帆顶角且拉紧帆后缘。

Sprit on: tight leech
斜撑杆拉紧：帆后缘变紧

Sprit off: loose leech
斜撑杆松开：帆后缘变松

Clew Outhaul 横拉器

Besides flattening the foot, the clew outhaul moves the leech away from the mast, opening the leech and flattening the sail.

除了让帆底边变平之外，帆尾角横拉器也会让帆后缘远离桅杆，打开帆后缘且让帆变平。

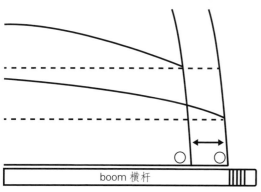

The clew outhaul flattens the sail and opens the leech

帆尾角横拉器让帆变平且打开帆后缘

Top Horizontal Tie, Tack Horizontal Tie, Luff Ties
顶部水平绑帆绳，帆前角水平绑帆绳，帆前缘绑帆绳

These alter the luff curve, which controls entry and fullness.

这些改变了帆前缘的弧度、控制风角和帆的饱满度。

Top Diagonal Tie, Tack Diagonal Tie (Boom Jaw Uphaul)
顶部斜向绑帆绳，帆前角斜向绑帆绳（横杆夹绳器上拉器）

These control luff length (entry and sail shape), position the sail on the mast, and control luff tension. The top diagonal tie stops the throat of the sail moving up the mast when the sprit tackle is tightened. The tack diagonal tie controls the height of the boom. It is shortened by twisting it the required number of times before hooking it onto its pin.

这些控制帆前缘的长度（风角和帆形），将帆与桅杆连接，并且控制帆前缘的松紧度。顶部斜向绑帆绳防止拉紧斜撑杆时上帆角上移，高过桅杆。帆前角斜向绑帆绳控制横拉器的高度。固定之前，可以通过缠绕所需圈数来缩短其长度。

Kicking Strap (Vang)
斜拉器

This holds the boom down offwind, tensions the leech and the luff as far as the diagonal tie allows, and counters the vertical push of the sprit. If the sprit is tightened before the kicking strap, the top of the luff will form loose folds. In light weather when the luff is slack, virtually no kicking strap tension is needed. In medium weather the kicking strap should be just slack when close-hauled, but tight enough to control sail twist offwind. In heavy weather it must be tight to tension the luff and maintain leech tension when the sail is spilled.

斜拉器将横杆往下拉，在斜向绑帆绳允许的范围内，拉紧帆后缘和帆前缘，并抵消斜撑杆的纵向推力。如果在调整斜拉器之前拉紧了斜撑杆，帆前缘的顶部会形成松散的褶皱。在小风天，当帆前缘松弛时，几乎不需要拉斜拉器。在中风天，斜拉器应该在迎风角度时刚好松弛，但在顺风航行时需要足够紧以控制帆的卷曲。在大风天，斜拉器必须拉紧，通过帆前缘和帆后缘变紧来卸力。

CHAPTER 2 第二章　　Sail & Rig 帆和索具

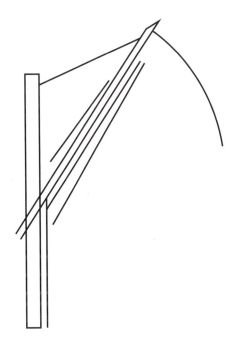

Tight sprit with no kicking strap (vang)
斜撑杆拉紧，不拉斜拉器

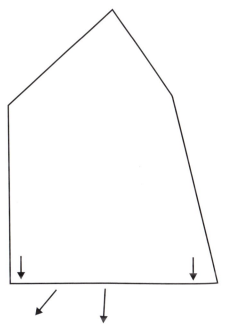

The kicking strap and mainsheet tighten the leech and the luff
斜拉器和主帆缭绳收紧帆后缘和帆前缘

Setting Up The Rig
装配索具

Tie the sail ties to the boom
用绑帆绳将帆绑在横杆上

Thread the mast through the mast sail ties (or tie the sail ties around the mast)
将桅杆穿过桅杆绑帆绳（或者将帆绑在桅杆上）

Attach the top horizontal tie and the top diagonal tie (see p24)
绑好顶部水平绑帆绳和顶部斜向绑帆绳（见第 18 页）①

---

①本书与原版图书页码有偏差，译文按本书页码。以下均同此处理。

Check the mast sail ties are the tension you want
确保桅杆绑帆绳是你想要的松紧度

Tie the tack horizontal tie
绑好帆前角水平绑帆绳

Attach the top of the sprit to the head of the sail
将斜撑杆的顶部与上帆边连接

By looping the rope around the button
环绕绳子把它扣上去

Attach the sprit tackle to the bottom of the sprit
将斜撑杆调节装置与斜撑杆底部连接

Put the mast up
举起桅杆

Attach the mast clamp to the mast thwart
将桅杆夹绑在桅座板上

Put the mast clamp on the mast and push it up snug to the thwart
将桅杆夹装上桅杆，并将其推至桅座板

Tighten the sprit tackle just enough to take the slack out of the top diagonal tie
拉紧斜撑杆，刚好足够将顶部斜向绑帆绳的松弛部分拉平

CHAPTER 2 第二章 | Sail & Rig 帆和索具

Set the luff tension by choosing how many twists of the tack diagonal tie (see p24/25)
以帆前角斜向绑帆绳的缠绕次数来设置帆前缘的松紧度（见第18/19页）

Rig the kicking strap
装斜拉器

Apply the kicking strap (vang) tension (holding the mainsheet tight makes this easier)
调节斜拉器（将主帆缭绳拉紧使其更容易调节）

Apply the desired amount of sprit tension
按需要拉紧斜撑杆

Adjust the outhaul
调节横拉器

Finally, check the sail is still within the bands
最后，检查帆的位置是否合适（在桅杆的标记内）

Boom Ties 横杆绑帆绳

Once you have set these up you will normally leave the boom attached to the sail and roll the sail around the boom when not using it.

一旦绑好，通常你会让帆与横杆保持连接的状态，当不用帆的时候，将帆卷在横杆上。

Mast Ties 桅杆绑帆绳

When using a sail for the first time you will tie these to the mast, thereafter you will thread the mast through them and then adjust the tension as required for the wind strength.

第一次使用帆的时候，将桅杆绑帆绳绑在桅杆上，然后把桅杆穿过它们，并根据风力调整松紧度。

Top Diagonal Tie 顶部斜向绑帆绳

This tie is important to get correct. It cannot be adjusted without taking the mast down. To calibrate the rig the tie should be adjusted to keep the top of the sail at the same height. The tie should be tensioned so that, when it is in tension and the luff is slack, the sail measurement band is just below the top mast measurement band. When maximum luff tension is applied the sail measurement band will be just above the lower mast measurement band.

正确设置这条绑帆绳十分重要。如果不将桅杆放下来，就无法调整。为了校准索具，应该调整这条绑帆绳以使帆的顶部保持在同一高度。

这条绑帆绳需要拉紧，拉紧时，帆前缘在松弛状态下，帆的丈量线刚好在桅杆上侧丈量线之下。当帆前缘拉到最紧时，帆的丈量线需要刚好在桅杆下侧丈量线之上。

> **DID YOU KNOW? 你知道吗？**
>
> The mark on the luff of the sail must be between the two measurement bands on the mast (see photo 18 on p23).
>
> The gap between the sail and the mast must not be more than 10 mm.
>
> 帆前缘上的标记必须在桅杆上的两条丈量线中间（见第17页的照片18）。帆和桅杆之间的距离不得超过10 mm。

Sail Shape For Different Wind Strengths
不同风力下的帆形

Every time you sail record your sail shape on a Race Training Analysis sheet (see p116), along with your comments on wind and sea conditions and how the boat performed. This helps to build up confidence, judgement and boatspeed.

每次航行时，都将你的帆形记录在竞赛培训训练分析表上（见第151页），以及你对风、海况和船的性能的判断。这有助于我们建立自信、判断力以及提高船速。

Light Wind Settings (Force 1–2 / 1–4 knots)
小风设置（1~2级/1~4节）

Slowly moving air will break away from a full sail, so aim to get a flat sail shape to prevent stalling and optimise acceleration / pointing. Aim for the maximum draft halfway back, with a slack luff and slack leech. You want a convex luff curve, flattening the draft and entry.

缓慢流动的空气无法流过饱满的帆，因此，应尽量保持一个较平的帆形，以防止失速，并优化加速/角度。以最大深度点在靠后一半的位置、松弛的帆前缘和帆后缘为目标。你想要一个凸出的帆前缘弧形、深度和风角变平。

- Top horizontal tie / tack horizontal tie—set at 9 mm gaps.
- 顶部水平绑帆绳/帆前角水平绑帆绳——间距设置为9 mm。
- Centre luff tie—no gap, but other luff ties set to give an evenly curved luff.
- 中间帆前缘绑帆绳不要留空隙，其他帆前缘绑帆绳设置为提供均匀的有弧度的帆前缘。
- Luff tension slack—put 3-4 twists in the loop of the tack diagonal tie, lifting the boom. With the luff slack the draft moves back and the entry flattens.
- 帆前缘松弛，帆前角斜向绑帆绳缠绕3~4次，将横杆抬起。帆前缘松弛，最大深度点后移且风角变平。
- Outhaul—pull out tight, which flattens sail.
- 拉紧横拉器，让帆变平。
- Kicking strap (vang)—totally slack so the leech is free to open.
- 斜拉器完全放松，帆后缘完全打开。
- Sprit—slacken until a small crease appears at the throat. This shows you are not over-spritted and the leech is open.
- 斜撑杆放松，直到上帆角位置出现一条小褶皱。这意味着你的斜撑杆没有过紧，帆后缘处于打开的状态。
- Boom jaws—must be tight on the mast but must allow the boom to lift as leech tension increases.
- 横杆固定绳，必须紧紧固定在桅杆上，但是必须允许帆后缘变紧时横杆上抬。

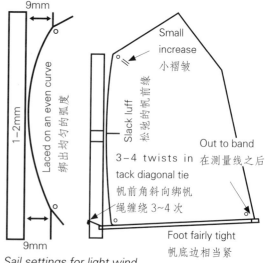

Sail settings for light wind
小风天帆的设置

Gusty Winds In All Conditions
各种情况下的阵风情况

Always set up your rig, and particularly the sprit, for the lighter wind in the lulls rather than the stronger winds in the gusts. When a gust comes it will open the leech and you will be able to sail through it. A rig with correct sprit and leech tension for the gusts will have a tight hooked leech in the lulls—deadly!

保持你的帆设置正确，尤其是斜撑杆，以适应小风情况，而不是阵风时的强风。阵风到来的时候，它会打开帆后缘，你就能穿过它。阵风情况下，正确设置的斜撑杆和帆后缘会在风间歇时使帆后缘偏紧。

Don't let the leech hook when there is a lull in the wind: adjust the sail shape for the lulls and accept that the leech will open in the gusts
有小风区时不要让帆后缘过紧：调整适应小风航行的帆形，接受帆后缘在阵风时打开

Full Power Settings (Force 2-4+ / 4-11+ knots)
中等风设置（2~4级以上/4~11节以上）

Set the sail with a straight luff and loose foot.
将帆设置为帆前缘笔直而帆底边松弛。

- Luff lacings, top and tack horizontal ties—adjust them to give an even 3–4mm gap along the whole luff.
- 帆前缘绑帆绳、顶部和帆前角水平绑帆绳——调整整个帆前缘使其距离桅杆3~4 mm的间距。
- Outhaul—ease so there are slight scallops in the foot between the boom ties. If the foot is too slack the leech hooks.
- 横拉器松开，以使帆底边的横杆绑帆绳之间有轻微的扇形褶皱。如果帆底边太松，帆后缘就会变紧。
- Kicking strap (vang)—just slack when the main is sheeted going upwind.
- 斜拉器——迎风航行主帆拉紧时刚好松弛。
- Sprit—as for light winds with a small crease at the throat.
- 斜撑杆——小风时在上帆角处有小小的褶皱。
- Luff tension—adjust by taking off enough twists from the tack diagonal tie to firm the luff. As the wind increases the luff must be tightened.
- 帆前缘——通过从帆前角斜向绑帆绳处解下足够的缠绕圈数来调节。风力增加时，必须收紧帆前缘。

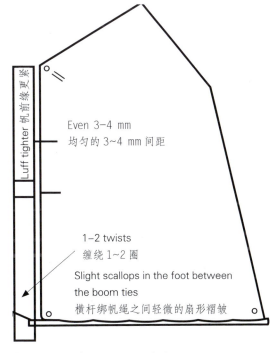

Sail settings for stronger wind
调整帆以适应更大风力

Heavyweights 大风

Heavy sailors can carry powered-up sails until racing is abandoned. The mast will bend, and to maintain the shape and power of the sail it is necessary to set up the top and tack horizontal ties tightly and ease the central luff ties to give an even curve with a middle lacing gap of about 9 mm.

体重较重的水手能够驾驭一面动力十足的帆，直到比赛结束。桅杆会弯曲，为了保持帆的形状和力量，有必要将顶部和帆前角水平绑帆绳绑得足够紧，适当调松中间帆前缘绑帆绳，以得到一个均匀的弧度，中间间距约 9 mm。

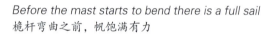

Before the mast starts to bend there is a full sail
桅杆弯曲之前，帆饱满有力

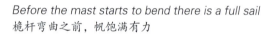

When the mast bends, the sail becomes flatter
桅杆弯曲时，帆面变得更平

Depowering 减力

You need to take another look at the rig if you're hiking hard with the daggerboard raised 10 cm and raked back but you are still spilling wind in the gusts and on wave tops and are finding it difficult to keep the boat driving without heeling.

如果在稳向板提起 10 cm 并向后倾斜的情况下，你仍然在非常努力地压舷，在阵风或浪尖时你仍在让帆减力，而且你发现很难让船在不倾斜的情况下航行，此时，你需要考虑调帆。

- Lace all luff ties with the eyelets with the luff of the sail just touching the mast.
- 帆前缘绑帆绳让帆刚好贴在桅杆上。
- Move the leech as far away from the mast as possible by tightening the outhaul to pull the clew to the black band. This flattens the lower half of the sail.
- 通过拉紧横拉器，将帆后角往黑色标记线之后拉，以使帆后缘尽量远离桅杆。这可以将帆的下半部分拉平。
- Ease the top horizontal tie to give an 8mm gap. This flattens the upper half of the sail. Allow for stretch—the maximum gap allowed is 10mm. Top ties must be very strong. They take all the sprit pull along the headrope as well as the sail's pull. They do most of the mast bending, and if they break the sail can tear.
- 将顶部水平绑帆绳放松至 8 mm 的间距。这可以将帆的上半部分拉平。允许拉伸——允许的最大的间距是 10 mm。顶部绑帆绳必须非常结实。它承受所有斜撑杆的拉力和帆的拉力。它们造成大部分的桅杆弯曲，如果断开，帆可能会撕裂。
- Tack horizontal tie must be tight.
- 帆前角水平绑帆绳必须绑紧。
- Luff must be as tight as possible. Heavyweights depower with evenly spaced luff lacings, as mast bend is flattening the entry for them.
- 帆前缘必须尽可能紧。体重较重的水手通过均匀间隔的帆前缘绑帆绳来减力，随着桅杆弯曲，使得风角变平。
- The kicking strap (vang) is important upwind to maintain leech tension when the wind is spilt. Apply as much tension as possible.
- 斜拉器在迎风航行时用于保持帆后缘的张力，斜拉器在迎风航行时对于保持帆后缘张力十分重要，当有风时尽可能拉紧。
- Sprit must be as tight as possible, except for lightweights who, if they are really struggling, can let the sprit off so the head of the sail flaps in the gusts. Experiment with how much sprit to let off. Too much and the boat won't point, too little and it will be hard to sail flat and want to go head to wind.
- 斜撑杆必须尽可能紧，除非是体重较轻的水手，他们真的在挣扎航行。他们可以松掉斜撑杆，让上帆边在阵风时飘动。尝试斜撑杆要松掉多少。如果松太多，船的角度上不去，松太少，很难保持船的平衡，船会迎风偏转。

CHAPTER 2 第二章 | Sail & Rig 帆和索具

To depower use a tight outhaul, tight sprit, tight luff and tight kicking strap (vang)
拉紧横拉器、斜撑杆、帆前缘和斜拉器来减力

CHAPTER 3 第三章
Upwind Speed 迎风船速

The main components for good upwind speed are:
好的迎风船速的主要组成部分是：
- Boat set-up
- 调船
- Steering
- 控舵
- Body movement
- 身体动作

To be the quickest upwind all of these need to be in sync and working together. Let's look at how we combine these elements to produce that blistering speed in different wind conditions and sea states.

想要获得最快的迎风速度，这些因素都需要同步并协同作用。我们来看一下如何将这些因素结合起来，在不同的风况和海况之下产生强劲的速度。

Smooth Water
平静水域

Light Wind 小风

Imagine the water has just the smallest ripples. The wind is drifting slowly across the sail. If the sail jerks, the air flow will break away and may take as long as one minute to adhere to the sail again. During that minute you have no drive! So, the key to fast light-wind sailing is sitting absolutely still and concentrating on keeping the sail pulling by accurate steering to the slightest twitch of the telltales. Feel the wind on your cheek and look for signs of the wind on the water so that you can anticipate any changes. All your movements must be slow and smooth, whether the sheet, the tiller or your body.

想象一下，水面只有微小的涟漪。风在帆上缓缓流动。如果猛拉帆，气流就会被打散，可能需要一分钟的时间来让气流重新聚集在帆上。在这一分钟的时间里，你没有动力！所以，

小风快速航行的关键是保持身体的绝对静止，集中注意力于通过精确控制舵保持帆上的力量，保持气流线的极小的抖动。感受脸颊上的风，寻找水面上风的迹象，这样你就能预料任何变化。你的所有动作都必须缓慢而流畅，不论是缭绳、主舵柄还是你的身体。

Boat set-up: The sail must be set up as flat as possible so that the slow-moving air flows over it without breaking away. A full sail only has a fraction of the drive of a flat sail in drifting conditions since the air flow separates from the back half of the sail for much of the time, and total separation (stalling) occurs more easily.

调船： 帆必须设置得尽可能平，这样缓慢移动的气流能够顺利流过帆，而不会被分散。小风情况，饱满的帆上的力量只是平的帆上力量的一部分，因为大部分时间气流从帆的后半部分分离，并且更容易发生完全分离的情况（失速）。

CHAPTER 3 第三章　**Upwind Speed 迎风船速**

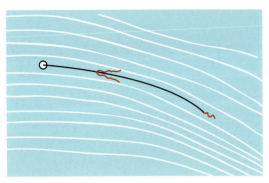

Slow air over a flat sail—all telltales (in red) are blowing back
缓慢的气流流过较平的帆——所有的气流线（红色）被往后吹

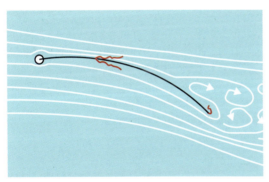

Slow air over a full sail—the flow has broken away from the back of the sail
缓慢的气流流过饱满的帆——气流在帆的后半部分散开

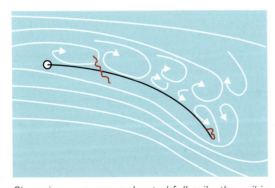

Slow air over an over-sheeted full sail—the sail is stalled with the flow totally broken away
缓慢的气流流过一面拉得过紧的饱满的帆——气流完全分散开，帆不工作

Set up as already mentioned with mast back (to give a little rudder feel / weather helm), outhaul tight, luff slack, sail ties loose and the luff in a smooth convex curve; the leech must be slack, so set the sprit tension loose enough to get small creases at the throat.

正如前文所述，船只装配时，桅杆后倾（制造轻微的舵感／上风舵），横拉器拉紧，帆前缘松弛，绑帆绳较松，帆前缘呈现平滑的凸出的弧度，帆后缘松弛，将斜撑杆调得足够松，以使上帆角处有小小的褶皱。

A thin lightweight or tapered mainsheet makes sail handling easier, and sensitivity can be further increased by dropping the purchase down to a 2:1.

一名苗条的体重较轻的水手或者逐渐变细的主缭会让控帆更容易，并且可以通过变成 2:1 来提升敏感度。

Steering: Keep tiller movements smooth and really concentrate on keeping the air flowing over the sail. Remember to keep the boat moving at all costs. It is tactically more important to keep in the wind patches than to sail on lifts so, if your patch is fading, head for the next one.

控舵：保持主舵柄的动作平稳，集中注意力于保持帆上气流的流动。记住要不惜一切代价保持船速。保持在风区比上升在战术上更为重要，如果风区快消失，就去找下一个。

Body movement: It may be necessary to heel the boat to leeward, so the sail holds its shape and the boom does not fall towards the centreline. Find a comfortable position—perhaps sitting on the bottom of the boat with your feet down to leeward keeping wind resistance down or, if the wind is a little more changeable, then squatting in the centre with your weight on the leeward foot so you can easily change your balance.

身体动作：可能有必要将船往下风倾斜，这有助于保持帆形，横杆不会摆向船的中心线。找到一个舒服的姿势——也许是坐在船里，双脚伸向下风，以此减小风的阻力，或者如果风稍微多变，蹲在中间，重心放在下风处的双脚上，

23

这样你可以轻易地改变平衡。

Make sure you are far enough forward to keep the transom out of the water, or eddies will form behind and slow you down. Dipping the bow does not matter if there are no waves and the boat isn't producing too big a bow wave.

确保你坐得足够靠前，以保持船尾脱离水面，否则船尾会产生乱流，让你减速。没有浪的情况，船不会产生太大的船头浪，船头下沉也没有那么重要。

Don't be negative if you are heavy. Heavy sailors have won championship races in these conditions and if you can get counting results you will be in a good position when the wind does come—in light airs the positive thinker wins!

如果你体重较大，也不要灰心丧气。体重较重的水手在这些情况下也赢得过冠军，如果你能够保持稳定发挥，风到来的时候，你就会处于较好的位置。风小时，积极的思考者会获得胜利！

Medium Wind 中风

The wind is strong enough to hold the boom to leeward, you are sitting on the side and starting to use the toestraps. The key is to have the boat in perfect balance so drag is reduced and be very accurate on your telltails.

风力足够让横杆保持在下风，水手坐在船舷上，开始使用压舷带。关键是保持船只处于完美的左右平衡状态，这样阻力减小，风向线也会非常准确。

Boat set-up: The mast can now go forward to keep the boom parallel to the hull, the sail can be deepened to give more power as the air flows more easily around the sail, so ease the outhaul. Before the race, get someone to check that your leech is not hooked. If your boat is slow, the leech will almost certainly be the problem, so adjust the sprit to get the small throat crease, check the kicking strap (vang) is slack and take off a twist from the tack diagonal tie to tighten the luff a little. You will be able to sheet the sail the hardest of all in these conditions allowing you to point high in the flat water.

调船：此时桅杆可以前倾，保持横杆与船体平行，因为此时气流更容易流过帆，帆面可以更深，以提供更多的力量，所以将横拉器调松。开始比赛之前，找人帮忙确认帆后缘并未过紧。如果你的船速很慢，最可能有问题的地方就是帆后缘，调整斜撑杆让上帆角处有小小的褶皱，确保斜拉器自然紧，帆前角斜向绑帆绳解开一圈，将帆前缘变紧一点。在这样的条件下，你需要将帆拉到最紧，以使你可以在平静水面小角度航行。

Steering: Concentrate on the telltails, try to keep them both flowing. If you get a small increase in breeze, see if you can just get the windward telltail to lift slightly so you can point even higher—but don't over do it and let the boat slow. Accurate steering to the wind is critical in these conditions.

控舵：集中注意力于风向线，试着让它们都平行飘动。如果风力稍微加大，看你是否能让上风风向线上扬一点，这样你的角度可以更高，但是不要太多，否则船速反而变慢。在这些条件下，准确地控舵至关重要。

Sailing upwind in light wind on flat water
平静水域小风天迎风航行

CHAPTER 3 第三章 | **Upwind Speed 迎风船速**

Sailing upwind in medium wind
中风迎风航行

Body movement: You are aiming to keep the boat trimmed with a slight heel to windward to keep the rudder from having weather helm. Drag from the rudder must be kept to a minimum. Sit on the side with your knees and feet together. Your feet should be ready to slip under the toestraps as the wind increases. Concentrate on your movement to keep the heel constant through the gusts and lulls, hitting the toestraps in a gust or sliding your bottom inside the gunwale in a lull. You will need to sit forward with your front leg against the bulkhead to keep the transom from dragging. When small waves start forming and splashing up the bow it's time to sit further back and sail the waves!

身体动作： 目标是保持的平衡，微微有一点向上风倾斜，防止上风舵现象。舵上的阻力必须保持在最小的程度。坐在船舷上，膝盖和双脚并拢。你的双脚应该时刻准备好，风力加大时，立刻放到压舷带下面。集中注意力于你的动作，保持阵风和小风区时持续的倾斜度，阵风时，运用你的压舷带，小风区时，将你的屁股移到船舷内侧去。你需要往前坐，将你靠近船头的腿靠在隔板上，以防止船尾的阻力。当小浪开始形成，拍打在船身时，你就需要往后坐，开始乘风破浪了！

Heavy Weather 大风

You are now overpowered; you need to work really hard to keep the boat flat and going fast. In stronger wind the sailor needs to take control of the boat and work hard.

现在你帆上的力量过大，你需要非常努力保持船只平衡和快速航行。风力较强时，水手需要非常努力地控制船。

Boat set-up: You now have more power being generated from the sail than you need. To lose some of that power start flattening the sail:

调船： 现在帆上获得的力量超过你所需要的。通过将帆变平一些来泄掉部分力量：

- Pull the outhaul tighter
- 将横拉器拉得更紧
- Take some twists off the tack diagonal tie to tighten the luff
- 帆前角斜向绑帆绳解掉一些，拉紧帆前缘
- Tighten the kicking strap (vang) so that when you let the mainsheet out the boom doesn't go upwards
- 拉紧斜拉器，这样当你松帆时，横杆不会向上移动
- Tighten the sprit so there are no creases
- 拉紧斜撑杆，去掉帆上褶皱

The loads on the main will be higher so the mast will start to bend. Adjust the mast rake so that the boom remains parallel to the boat and the overall balance remains the same. If you are

25

struggling with weather helm in the gusts, then try lifting the daggerboard by up to 25 cm. This should reduce the weather helm and the heeling moment, making the boat easier to sail.

帆上的力量加大，因此桅杆会开始变弯。调整桅杆倾斜度，让横杆仍然与船保持平行，也保持整体的平衡不变。如果阵风时你被上风舵困扰，试着将稳向板提起 25 cm。这应该能减轻上风舵以及船的倾斜，让船更易操控。

When it gets towards survival conditions, and especially for the lighter helms, start letting the sprit off. This will look horrible but will open the leech and reduce the power dramatically. You won't point as well but at least you will be going forwards!

进入"保命"阶段的时候，尤其是对于体重较轻的水手，开始松掉斜撑杆。这看上去很可怕，但是可以打开帆后缘，大幅地泄力。你的角度不会很好，但是至少你还在向前航行！

Steering: You are now steering to keep the boat flat, pinching to take power out of the sail. As you get a gust, hike hard and flat. If you are still overpowered, then pinch slightly or, if the boat is slowing, release the sail slightly by easing the sheet by straightening your arm. As the gust goes then power the boat up by bearing away slightly and pulling the main back in. The main focus is to keep the boat flat.

控舵：现在你需要掌舵以保持船是平的，通过小角度迎风航行，以减小帆上的力量。当阵风到来的时候，用力压舷保持船的平衡。如果仍然力量过大，稍微迎风偏转一点，如果船速变慢，通过伸直手臂松缭绳来稍微松点帆。阵风过去的时候，稍微顺风偏转一点，拉紧一点帆以增加力量。主要的关注点是保持船是平的。

Body movement: A lot of the body movement and position will be covered in the wave sailing section (p32). Remember the more you hike, the more leverage and the faster you go! Your toestraps should be set so your thighs are parallel to the boat and the gunwale is halfway along the back of your thighs. Hold the end of the tiller extension so your arm is bent, and you can still steer while sat out hard. Your mainsheet hand should be held high so you can play the sheet in the gusts without changing your grip. Keep the boat driving at speed on the beat, hiking well out in a position you can comfortably keep up for the whole race. You then have a little in reserve for short periods of extreme effort in gusts or critical moments of the race.

身体动作：浪中航行部分（第 29 页）将涉及许多身体动作和位置。记住，压舷越多，杠杆越大，航行得越快！你的压舷带应该设置为让你的大腿与船平行，大腿后侧的一半位置正好在船舷之上。握住副舵柄的末端，手臂弯曲，这样即使你用力压舷的时候也可以继续控舵。握缭绳的手应该高一些，这样阵风到来的时候，你可以在不调整握的地方的情况下调整缭绳。保持迎风段船快速行驶，保持一个可持续整场比赛的舒服的压舷姿势。然后你就有了一点储备，应对比赛中的阵风或关键时刻的短期极度努力。

Have your body upright in the lulls
小风区时身体坐直

Extend your body in the gusts
阵风时舒展身体

Extending fully when required
需要时完全舒展

CHAPTER 3 第三章 | Upwind Speed 迎风船速

> **TOP TIPS 几点建议**
>
> **Heavy Weather Upwind**
> 大风迎风航行
> The sail must be depowered. Set with tight luff, tight lacings, eased top tie, very tight sprit and kicking strap (vang).
> 帆应该减力。帆前缘收紧,绑帆绳收紧,放松顶部绑帆绳,斜撑杆非常紧,斜拉器非常紧。
> All except lightweights, keep the outhaul slack 1 cm to drive through the waves.
> 除了体重较轻的水手之外,将横拉器保持 1 cm 的间距,以便在海浪中行驶。
> Sit well back to lift the bow.
> 往后坐,让船头抬起。
> Heel 5 degrees to lift the weather bow.
> 向下倾斜 5 度,让上风船头抬起。
> Hike hard and drive the boat. Spill wind in the gusts, don't luff.
> 用力压舷,让船航行。阵风时泄力,而非迎风偏转。
> In lulls sheet in, lean in, bail when you can but keep moving.
> 小风区时,拉帆,身体往里,有机会时舀水出去,但要保持航行状态。
> Sail free and fast. All except heavyweights will go to windward with the boom end well outside the back corner of the boat.
> 自由快速航行。除了体重较重的水手之外,都需要坐在上风舷,保持横杆末端在船尾角之外。
> Maintain boat balance by lifting the daggerboard by up to 25 cm.
> 通过将稳向板上抬 25 cm 实现船只左右平衡。
> Think before tacking. Look for a smoother patch, and tack on top of a wave. It can be a nightmare if you tack into a steep wave.
> 迎风换舷前仔细思考。选择一个平稳一些的区域,在浪上换舷。如果你迎风换舷进入一个巨浪,那可能是一场噩梦。
> Getting stuck in 'irons' during a tack is a disaster. The boat stops and then starts blowing backwards. To get out of it, point the rudder in the direction you want the stern to go, and lift the daggerboard three-quarters of the way up. When you are on a reach, begin to pull the mainsail in and sit out to get forward momentum again.
> 换舷时卡在不可航行角度,就是一个灾难。船会停下来,然后被风吹着开始倒退。摆脱不可航行角度,将你的舵指向你想让船尾去的方向,并且将稳向板抬起四分之三。当你到横风角度时,开始拉帆,坐出去,再次获得往前的动力。
> To get home in a 'hurricane', take down the sprit and sail in on the bottom half of the mainsail.
> 想要在"飓风"中回家,取下斜撑杆,用帆的下半部分航行。

Bailing
舀水

Keeping water out of the boat is essential to fast heavy wind sailing but it is inevitable you will ship some water in heavy winds.

船里干燥对于快速航行至关重要,但是在大风时不可避免地会有水进船。

Bailing is vital in heavy weather. If you can't keep your boat dry you will not survive the race! Fill a bucket with water and feel how heavy it is. Then pour it into your boat. It will spread out until it's hardly noticeable! If a few buckets of water are sloshing around they will make the boat heavy; she will not lift so well to waves; more water will break on board; and she will be harder to steer and keep upright. The weight of water to leeward counterbalances your hiking, the boat heels more, and weather helm gets extreme.

舀水在大风时至关重要。如果无法保持船内干燥，你就无法在比赛中生存！把水桶装满水，感受它的重量，然后将它倒进船里，水会散开，直到几乎看不见为止！如果几桶水在船里晃荡，就会让船变重。它不会很好地随着浪的上升而上升，更多的浪会拍在船上，让船变得更难控制和保持直立。下风侧的水的重量抵消了你的压舷作用，船倾斜得更厉害，上风舵也变得极大。

Bail early: as soon as you have any noticeable water in your boat. Don't wait until you have slowed from the weight. Remember that the more water that gets in the boat, the quicker water will come in.

尽早舀水：只要你的船上有任何明显的水，不要等到你的船速已经因此变慢。记住，船里的水越多，水进来的速度就会越快。

Do not stop the boat to bail. If the boat is kept sailing, however slowly, when you are bailing, you will not slip to leeward:

不要为了舀水将船停下来。如果船在保持航行，不论多慢，当你舀水时，你都不会滑到下风去：

- Ease the main enough to get the boat heeling to windward
- 松足够的帆，让船向上风倾斜
- Move back until you have enough space to bail in front of your leg
- 往后移动，直到你有足够的空间在你的腿部前侧舀水
- Keep your backside well out over the side
- 保持你的身体后侧在船边上
- Lean in and scoop forward towards the bulkhead
- 身体往里倾，向前往隔板舀水

While keeping the boat moving, heel slightly to windward and fill up the bailer
船往前航行的时候，稍微向上风倾斜，装满水舀

Chuck out the water while keeping moving
船继续航行，将水倒掉

Use the helm to keep the boat moving smoothly ahead and a little upwind, luffing if the sail threatens to heel the boat and bearing off if the main lifts or the boat slows too much.

利用控舵来保持船只平稳地向前航行和轻微地迎风偏转，如果帆上的力量即将让船倾斜，进行迎风偏转，如果帆上力量变小或船速变得过慢，进行顺风偏转。

Power Bailing 强力排水

Now try sailing more sheeted, taking advantage of lulls in the wind or the troughs of the waves to lean in rapidly and scoop without losing any boatspeed. You will eventually find that, with tiller and main in one hand, you can luff a little while hiking, and make the water cross the boat in a little wave. You can then lean in quickly and take a scoop as the water reaches the weather side, then lean out hard while bearing off, powering the boat up and over the next wave as you dump the water.

现在，试着将帆拉得更紧继续航行，利用小风区或者通过浪的时候，身体快速往里，在不损失任何速度的情况下快速舀水。最终你会发现，一手拿着副舵柄和缭绳，压舷时可以迎风偏转一点，让船里的水在浪小的时候到对面来。然后你可以在水到达上风侧时迅速进去，舀水，然后在顺风偏转时用力往外压，给船加力，并在下一个浪时，将水倒掉。

Lean in and get a scoop in a lull
小风区时身体往里，舀水

Hike hard when you dump the water
倒水时用力压舷

And keep sailing fast
然后继续快速航行

Sailing In Waves
浪中航行

Basic Principles 基本原则

Many styles of wave sailing can be seen at international events. Different wave conditions pose different problems, but two basic principles always apply:

在国际赛事中可以看到很多风格的浪中航行。不同的海浪情况带来不同的问题，但两个基本原则始终适用：

- It is vital that speed is maintained and as little of the boat's dynamic energy as possible is lost negotiating each wave
- 保持速度是至关重要的，并在每次海浪中尽可能少地损失船只的动力
- Energy loss occurs when the boat and helm are slowed by pitching, by sailing uphill and by wave impact on the bow or helm
- 当上下颠簸、上浪时，船头或舵受海浪影

OPTIMIST RACING OP 级帆船竞赛

响时，船速减慢，动力损失

Pitching 上下颠簸

When a boat goes through waves, the ends of the boat move up and down. This is called pitching and this movement absorbs driving energy and slows the boat down. The more easily the ends can lift, the less energy will be lost. This can be achieved by:

当船只在穿过海浪时，船的两端会上下移动。这就是我们所说的上下颠簸，这个动作会吸收前进的动力，使船减速。两端越容易被抬起，损失的能量就越少。这可以通过以下方式实现：

- Keeping the ends of the boat as light as possible. Food, drink, sponges, painters and paddles should all be stowed by the daggerboard box.
- 让船的两端尽可能轻。食物、饮料、海绵、船头绳、桨都应该被放在稳向板槽附近。
- Sitting at the point where the boat pivots, so the boat moves without moving your body. Only the boat pitches—you maintain your equilibrium and less energy is lost.

Allow your body to move with the motion of the boat, keep your core muscles relaxed and flexible. On larger waves you can help the bow rise by more forcefully rocking your shoulders back then returning to your equilibrium position.

- 坐在船的旋转中心上，这样船可以在你不移动身体的情况下移动。只有在船上下颠簸时，你保持平衡，才能减少能量损失。让你的身体随着船的运动而运动，保持核心肌肉放松和灵活。在大浪情况下，你可以通过更有力地向后摆动肩膀，然后回到平衡位置，来帮助抬起船头。

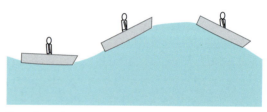

To reduce the energy lost, allow the boat to pitch
为了减少动力损失，允许船进行上下颠簸

Sailing in Waves 浪中航行

As you go down the wave
下浪时

Bear away down the wave
顺风偏转跟着海浪下去

And lean back
然后往外压

CHAPTER 3 第三章　　Upwind Speed 迎风船速

So the bow rises
船头抬起

To the top of the wave
至浪的顶部

Go for maximum power
获得最大的动力

As you begin to go down
当你开始往下时

Bearing away
顺风偏转

To speed up down the wave
加速下浪

Apart from the loss of energy and speed when pitching due to the hull moving up and down there is another effect. The rig will also rock backwards and forwards. The apparent wind moves forward as the rig rocks forward down a wave and, as the bow rises and the rig rocks back, the apparent wind moves backwards. This means that the sail is never set at the optimum angle causing loss of power and speed.

船上下颠簸的时候，由于船体上下移动，除了动力和速度的损失之外，还有另外一个影响——帆也会前后摆动。下浪时帆向前摆动，视风向前移动，当船头抬起，帆向后摆动时，视风向后移动。这意味着帆永远不会在一个最佳角度，导致动力和速度的损失。

This isn't too much of a problem once you are overpowered because you can adjust to this with steering and playing the main. However, in lighter winds and big waves or chop, it can mean that, when trying to stop the boat pitching, it is better to keep the power in the sail and accept the loss from hitting the waves.

帆上力量过大时，这不会是一个多大的问

31

OPTIMIST RACING OP 级帆船竞赛

题,因为你可以通过控舵和调帆来调整。然而,在风小、浪大或者汹涌的情况,这可能意味着,想要试图阻止船上下颠簸,更好的选择是保持帆上的力量,并接受海浪造成的损失。

In these conditions you move your body the opposite way and, as the wave tries to lift the bow, you rock forward to try to push it down to keep the sail more stationary.

在这种情况下,反向移动你的身体。当海浪试图抬起船头时,身体往前将它压下去,这会让帆处于相对静止的状态。

你可以通过控舵尽量减少上浪的时间:海浪抬起你的船头时迎风偏转,在海浪顶部时,顺风偏转并加速。这就是借力。当你达到浪顶并加速时,尽可能用力地将船压平。然后在波谷中短暂地休息一下,在下一个浪上迎风偏转。

Head up as the wave lifts your bow
海浪让船头抬起时迎风偏转

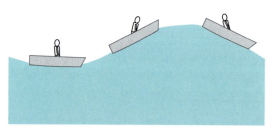

If you are trying to reduce pitching and the effect on the rig, move in the opposite way to the boat
如果你试图减轻上下颠簸以及对帆造成的影响力,那么身体向船的反方向移动

Uphill 上浪

Energy and speed are lost when the boat has to rise to go over a wave. In chop this isn't as much of a problem—pitching is more important. However, in larger waves, going up the face of the wave can slow you dramatically and cause lots of leeway.

当船不得不上升航行越过海浪时,动力和速度都会有损失。在小浪的水面上航行,这并非什么大问题——偏高航行才是。然而,在较大的海浪中,沿着海浪的表面上升会显著减慢速度,并造成明显的横移。

You can steer to minimise the time going up the wave: head up as the wave lifts your bow then, on the top of the wave, bear away and power up. This is called power beating. As you get to the top of the wave and pull the power on, hike the boat level as forcefully as you can. Then move in for the short lull in the trough and as you head up the face of the next wave.

Power up and bear away down the wave
加速并顺风偏转下浪

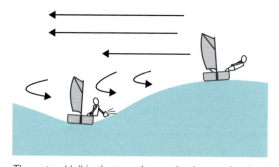

The natural lull in the trough can also be used to heel to weather and scoop out a bailer of water
在波谷中自然的小风区,也可以向上风倾斜并舀水一次

CHAPTER 3 第三章 | Upwind Speed 迎风船速

Wave Impact 海浪的影响

The impact of waves on the bow will kill boatspeed. The weather bow is particularly important because impact here results in water coming aboard.

海浪对船头的冲击会降低船速。上风船头尤为重要，因为这里的冲击会导致水进入船里。

- Sit back to lift the bow: sailors 45 kg or more sit 20 cm behind the bulkhead; smaller sailors sit up to 60 cm back in heavyweather
- 往后坐，抬起船头：体重45 kg及以上的水手坐在隔板向后20 cm的位置；体型较小的水手在大风天坐在隔板向后60 cm往后的位置
- Heel the boat 5 degrees to lift the weather bow
- 船向下倾斜5°，抬起上风船头
- Balance the boat by lifting the daggerboard
- 通过抬起稳向板来平衡船只
- Sail fast and free
- 航行得更快更自由
- Allow the boat to pitch easily
- 允许船上下颠簸

Wave impact on the helm can seriously stop the boat. It is important in waves to hike with your thighs parallel to the boat so your body doesn't get close to the water and you can see the waves.

海浪对舵的冲击可以让船完全停下。在海浪中航行，压舷时大腿与船平行是非常重要的，这样你的身体就不会靠近水，你就能看到海浪。

Wave conditions vary massively in size, shape and angle. When sailing in waves, the key is to work out which effect is the most detrimental to boatspeed and then deploy the best technique of set-up, steering, body movement and position to counter this. And remember waves are great fun!!

海浪的大小、形状和角度变化很大。当在海浪中航行时，关键是要找出对船速最不利的影响因素，然后运用最佳的设置、控舵、身体动作和姿势来应对这种影响。记住，海浪是非常有趣的！

Bad Habits 糟糕的习惯

Take a look at top competitors at an international event sailing to windward. Most will be storming along, hiking hard and appearing to be going fast. Take a closer look. While some are sailing with a smooth continuous motion, others sail fast then pause, slowing before getting back to full speed, then slow again.

观察一下国际赛事中迎风航行的顶级竞争对手。大多数都气势汹汹，努力压舷，看起来速度很快。当我们凑近观察的时候，会发现有些人航行的时候会伴随着持续的动作，另一些人则快速航行，然后失速，在下一次达到全速之前减速，然后再次减速。

Beware of burying the bow in chop—lean back to lift the bow over each wave
当心船头在汹涌的水面扎水向后压舷，每一次浪来的时候抬起船头

Take a look at your own sailing. Do you sail smoothly and at maximum speed, or are you a pauser? It's easy to pick up bad habits which are hard to recognise and change.

观察一下你自己的航行。你是以最快的速度平稳航行，还是你是一个会失速的人？我们很容易养成一些难以识别和改正的坏习惯。

- Do you luff too much in the gusts? Is this due to letting your boat heel too much? Should you be playing the mainsheet to keep her level?
- 阵风时是否迎风偏转太多？这是否是因为你让自己的船倾斜太多？你是否应该通过调整缭绳来让船保持平衡？
- Are you fit enough to drive fast and hard for a whole beat? Are your hiking pants comfortable?
- 你的体能是否足够支撑你一整个迎风段的快速和努力航行？你的压舷裤舒服吗？
- Are your feet supported firmly by the toestraps in the right places? Do you wriggle from one leg to the other, and what happens to the boat when you do this?
- 你的双脚被压舷带牢牢地支撑在正确的位置吗？你会两只脚来回替换吗？当你这样做时，船会发生什么？
- Do you really keep the boat level or is it heeled to leeward? It's easy to get used to an angle of heel which is comfortable, but it may make the boat unbalanced. How about trying an inclinometer on your mast thwart to help change your style?
- 你真的把船压平了吗？还是它向下风倾斜着？我们非常容易对一个倾斜度感到舒适，但这可能会让船不平衡。试试利用桅座板上的倾角仪来帮助你改变风格如何？
- Are you hitting waves with the bow or with your body?
- 你的船头或者身体在撞击海浪吗？

When you are training or racing, try to sail the boat at 100% focus and as well as you can. Avoid picking up bad habits.

当你在训练或者竞赛时，尽可能以100%的专注度来驾驶帆船。避免养成坏习惯。

PRACTICE IDEAS 训练计划

'Buddy' Training & Tuning
"伙伴"训练法和调船

In the Optimist class top sailors have often had more than a lifetime's worth of suggestions hollered at them by well-meaning parents and coaches. It is much better to work out problems and other aspects of tuning and boatspeed for yourself, and the way to do this is by buddy training.

在OP级别中，顶级水手往往会收到一些来自善意的父母和教练的可受益一生的建议。如果你能够自己找到你在调船和船速方面的问题，这是更好的，而做到这一点的方式是通过"伙伴"训练法。

Find a friend who is your size and about the same speed. Get into the habit of sailing together at every opportunity. Try different aspects of tuning, technique, daggerboard or mast rake, boat trim, and styles of hiking. Check out and criticise each other's sailing style and sail shapes, discussing settings for the day. If one of the boats is sailing like a drain, two heads are better than one to sort out the problems. Buddy tuning gives you confidence—on the day of the big race, after sailing for five minutes with your buddy, you will know your boat is as fast as ever.

找一个体型跟你差不多，速度也差不多的朋友。要养成一有机会就一起航行的习惯。尝试调船、技巧、稳向板或者桅杆倾斜度、前后平衡、压舷的风格等不同方面，观察并评判彼此的航行风格和帆形，讨论当日的设置。如果其中一艘船表现糟糕，"三个臭皮匠，顶个诸葛亮"，两个人能更好地解决问题。"伙伴"训练法能够给予你信心——在大型比赛

Similar techniques to buddy training can be used after the start. If you do not feel your boat is moving as she should, check a boat that is going well. What are they doing different? Check everything, then change something. Faster? Yes! Now sail away!

类似于"伙伴"训练法的技巧也可以运用在起航之后。如果你认为你的船速不佳，观察船速很好的那条船。它们做了什么不同的事？检查所有要素，然后做一定调整。变快了吗？是的！现在扬帆起航吧！

The standard procedure for buddy training is to sail on the same tack as your buddy, with the leeward boat slightly bow forward and the hulls two to four lengths apart. In this way, neither boat will be blanketed or backwinded by the other, and wash will not be a problem.

"伙伴"训练法的标准操作流程是与你的伙伴航行同一舷，下风船的船头稍微在前面一点，船体间距2~4倍船长。这样，两条船都不会被对方遮盖或造成脏风，船航行造成的水纹也不会是问题。

Sail like this until one boat draws ahead. Stop when the boat behind gets disturbed air or hits the wake. Cruise together and chat about it. Then try again, changing over the windward and leeward stations. If the same boat draws ahead, raft up and discuss why. If you can't work it out, get the slower boat sailing with the other skipper watching. If he can't spot the problem, change over with the slower helm watching the faster boat.

保持航行，直到其中一条船航行到前面。当后面的船受到乱流影响或者撞击海浪的时候停下，航行到一起并进行讨论。然后上下风船交换位置再试一次。如果还是同一条船航行到了前面，互相凑在一起，讨论原因。如果你们不能解决这个问题，让船速较慢的船航行，让船速较快的水手观察。如果他无法指出问题所在，两人交换，船速较慢的水手观察，船速较快的船航行。

You can also work on boat handling with 'follow-my-leader' sessions and try close covering team-race-style duels.

你也可以通过"跟船航行"课程和近距离队赛来练习控船技术。

Group Tuning 团队调船

Used by a group (with or without a coach) to check speed, pointing, sail setting, tune and technique. After a gate start, the boats aim to get three lengths apart, close-hauled on the same tack. After a while you will see that some boats are sailing higher and some faster. Stop, compare settings, discuss, adjust and try again—to get everyone sailing high and fast!

适用于团队（有或没有教练）用来检查船速、角度、帆的位置、调船和技术。门标起航之后，船与船之间分开3倍船长的距离，同一舷迎风航行。一段时间之后，你会发现有的船角度更好，有的船速度更快。停下来，对比设置，进行讨论，调整并再次尝试——让所有人的角度又好船速又快！

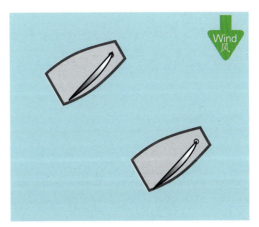

Positions for buddy training upwind
"伙伴"训练法迎风航行时的位置

CHAPTER 4 第四章
Downwind Speed 顺风船速

As with upwind speed, the main components for good downwind speed are:
和迎风船速一样，良好的顺风船速要素为：

- Boat set-up
- 船只设置
- Steering
- 掌舵
- Body movement
- 身体动作

The downwind should not be looked at as a rest before you have to go upwind again. You should not just bear away and point at the mark. Big speed and place gains can be made downwind by working the boat correctly. Let's look at some techniques you can use.

大家不应该将顺风航段看作是与下一个迎风段之间的休息阶段。这不仅仅是对准下风标的顺风偏转。如果能在这一航段采取合理的操作，就可以在顺风航段获得更快的船速并提高名次。让我们一起来看看都可以使用哪些技巧吧！

Smooth Water
水面平静

Light Wind 小风

Patience and concentration are required for long light-wind downwinds.
在小风天长时间顺风航行，需要水手有足够的耐心和专注力。

Boat set-up: It is important to set the kicking strap (vang) before the start for the downwind. It should be set so that, when running, it is slack enough that the leech is just opening in the gusts. You should be able to see the leech opening and closing on each gust and lull. Too little and the leech will just hang open, too much and it will remain continually closed and stalled.

船只设置： 在开始顺风航行前，提前设置好斜拉器非常重要。斜拉器应足够松弛，确保在顺风航行时，帆后缘刚好在阵风中打开。要能够看到帆后缘在每次遇到阵风和弱风时的打开和关闭。斜拉器收紧过少，帆后缘就会一直呈松弛状态；收紧过多，帆后缘会持续处于关闭状态，气流难以通过。

As you bear away onto a run, the pressure in the sail will reduce. This will mean the sprit will be too tight. You may have to lean forward and let it off slightly to avoid a crease running from the head to the tack.

随着你顺风偏转到顺风角度航行，帆上的受力会减小。这就意味着斜撑杆会过紧。你可能需要往前倾斜，稍微使斜撑杆松一点，避免上帆顶角和前帆角之间出现褶皱。

In light weather it is possible and desirable to sail downwind with the boom well forward of the mast. In this position, with the boat heeled to windward (kiting), gravity will hold the boom out. This can also help the light-weight sailor kite easier as the sail pushes the boat into windward heel.

在小风天顺风航行时，最好将横杆完全置于桅杆之前。在此位置，使船倾向上风（反压舷），重力会使横杆保持在船外侧。帆力会使船倾向上风侧，所以还能帮助体重较轻的水手更好地反压舷。

It is common to see Optimists going downwind with too much daggerboard.

驾驶 OP 顺风航行时，稳向板放下过多的情况很常见。

Roll your boat and take a look at how much daggerboard projects with your favourite downwind settings. On a light-wind smooth-water run the board should not project from the bottom of the boat at all.

滚动船体，看看需要提起多少稳向板以达到最佳顺风设置。在风小且水面平稳的情况下，稳向板应完全不插入船底。

Running in light winds with the daggerboard up
在小风天顺风航行，稳向板完全拉起

From above 俯视

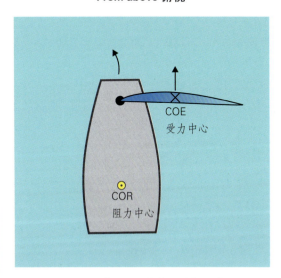

From astern 船尾

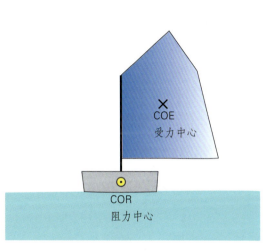

If you sail flat, the Centre of Effort (COE) of the sail is to the leeward side of the Centre of Resistance (COR) of the hull, so the boat luffs up

如果航行平稳，帆的受力中心（COE）位于船体阻力中心（COR）的下风侧，船会迎风偏转

37

OPTIMIST RACING OP 级帆船竞赛

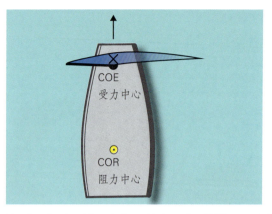 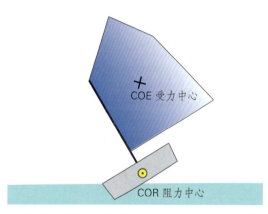

Heeling the boat to windward brings the COE more in line with the COR and the boat sails straight ahead with the rudder straight
使船倾向上风，能使受力中心和阻力中心与航行方向更加一致，保持船舵居中，船就会往前航行

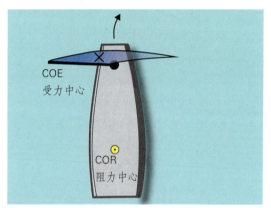 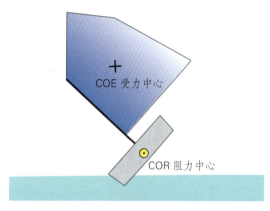

Heeling the boat too far to windward takes the COE to the windward side of the COR, so the boat bears away
如果船往上风倾斜过多，就会使受力中心位于阻力中心的上风侧，船就会顺风偏转

Correct kiting position
正确的反压舷位置

Kited too far, resulting in instability and using the rudder too much
反压舷过多，导致船体不稳和过量用舵

> **DID YOU KNOW? 你知道吗?**
>
> For every centimetre your board is raised, you decrease surface area by 58sqcm, and reduce water friction accordingly. Mark the back edge of the board at 10cm intervals for reference.
>
> 稳向板每提起1cm，板的接触面积就减小58cm²，水的阻力相应减少。可以在稳向板后侧以10cm 间隔进行标记，以作参考。

Steering: There should be no load on the rudder when on a light-wind run. The rudder should be following the boat. To achieve this the boat will have to be heeled on top of you (kited). To steer, use body weight and change the heel of the boat. More heel to windward to bear away and less heel to head up. Hold the tiller extension lightly and let the rudder follow where the boat wants to go.

掌舵：在小风天顺风航行时，船舵应不受任何力，舵要随船而动。为了实现此目的，应往身体上方滚动船体（反压舷）。利用体重和船的倾斜控制船的方向。更多地倾向上风，船就会顺风偏转；减少倾斜，船就会迎风偏转。轻握副舵柄，让舵跟随船的航行。

Body movement: Sit well forward against the bulkhead with your front knee pointing down the gunwale. Your other leg should be tucked underneath you. You should then be able to kite without holding onto the daggerboard for support. Your front hand should be holding the mainsheet to allow trimming to help balance.

身体动作：紧贴船舱壁靠前坐，前膝盖朝前紧贴船舷。另一条腿应收到身体下方，这样就不用在反压舷时抓住稳向板作为支撑了。前手应抓住主缭绳，以便进行调节，辅助船的平衡。

The most common mistake is to try to kite too much. This can result in wobbles and using the rudder to steer which slows the Optimist down.

最常见的错误操作是过度反压舷，这会导致船体不稳；过度用舵会降低船速。

Medium Wind 中风

The boat is now starting to move nicely downwind. Most of the light wind advice still applies but with some subtle differences.

当船开始顺畅地顺风行驶，大多数小风时候的建议仍然适用，但存在些微差别。

Boat set-up: The kicking strap (vang) is set up the same way as in light wind so that the leech is just opening in the gusts. The sail can be now be set at 90° to get maximum projected area since it is windy enough for the boom to stay out on its own. The sprit probably won't need letting off because there is enough wind so that the sail should keep its shape.

船只设置：斜拉器的设置和小风时候是一样的，这样能确保帆后缘刚好在阵风中打开。这样的话，帆就可以打开到90°，获得最大的受风面积。由于受风足够，可保持横杆在船外侧。斜撑杆也许不用松，因为有足够的风力保持帆的形状。

On the run, sit with your front knee pointing down the gunwale; do not hold the daggerboard
顺风航行坐姿：前膝盖往前紧贴船舷，不要抓稳向板

The daggerboard can still be raised all the way but if, as the wind increases, the boat becomes unstable then a little down will help. Still kite to reduce wetted surface area and drag.

稳向板仍可保持完全提起，但是如果风力

上升，船开始变得不稳定，稍微放下一点稳向板会有助于航行。继续反压舷，减小船的入水面积和阻力。

Steering: Continue to steer with body weight and let the rudder follow the boat.
掌舵：继续运用身体重量控制方向，让舵跟随船的移动。

Body movement: Slide slightly further back in the boat as the wind increases to stop the nose digging in. Correct fore-and-aft trim is critical to running speed:
肢体动作：随着风力上升，身体稍微往船后侧移动，以防船头扎入水中。合理的前后位置调节对于顺风速度至关重要：

- If you are too far forward, the bow digs in, kicking up a wave and increasing the wash. This can be risky for lightweights because it can lead to nose-diving and broaching.
- 如果你过于靠前，就会导致船头下沉，冲击海浪，激起更多浪花。这对于体重较轻的水手是很危险的，因为这会导致船头扎入水中，并使船体打横。
- If you are too far back, the water begins to bubble and eddy behind the transom. This is particularly damaging when you're sailing slowly. The water should slide away without a sign that the boat has passed.
- 如果你过于靠后，水流会开始在船尾处形成泡沫和涡流。尤其是在慢速航行时，对船速影响巨大。随着船的移动，水流应该要能不留痕迹地顺畅流过。

Heavyweights usually sink both the bow and stern and have to find a happy medium where drag is least. Lightweights can avoid bow and stern drag almost totally. Their problem is more one of getting back and out to keep the boat level with the bow lifting in the gusts.
体重较重的水手通常会导致船头和船尾均下沉，所以务必要找到一个适当的中间点，以确保船只所受阻力最小。体重较轻的水手基本上可以完全避免船头和船尾的阻力。他们更需要关注的是，当上风船头在阵风中被抬起时，往船后移动，往外压舷，保持船体的水平。

Kiting 反压舷

Mainsail at 90°, daggerboard up
主帆打开 90°，抬起稳向板

Let the mainsail out to increase the kiting
主帆松出去更多，增加反压舷

Watch the direction of the flow of the telltales
注意观察风向线飘起的方向

Lean back down the waves
顺浪航行，身体后倾

And as the roll increases
随着船体滚动更多

Trim the mainsheet in again to flatten the boat
再次收紧主缭，使船体平稳

Heavy Wind 强风

It takes a fair breeze to get an Optimist up and planing but, once they are away, they really travel. The big danger now is a nose-dive.

让OP开始滑行需要较强的风力，但是一旦开始，速度就会相当快。这种时候，主要的危险就是船头扎水。

Boat set-up: The kicking strap (vang) now has to be tight to keep the sail stable downwind without too much twist. Too slack and the head of the sail blows forward making a greater chance of nose-diving or the dreaded death roll.

船只设置：这时候，一定要收紧斜拉器，以保持帆在顺风航行时的平稳，且无过多扭曲。如果斜拉器过松，上帆边被风往前吹，会增加船头扎水的可能性，更甚者会发生正顺翻覆。

Bring the sail in slightly from the 90° to keep the boat more stable.

将帆从90°稍微往里收紧，提高船的稳定性。

The board should also not be pulled up as far to help with stability and allow more accurate and positive steering.

稳向板也不应抬起过高，来促进航行的稳向性，使掌舵更精准、更有效。

Steering: The boat now will not be sailed so directly downwind. The boat can be sailed slightly higher to get flow across the sail or run by the lee if it's not too unstable. Since it's windy you are likely to be encountering waves and need to steer to catch these. We will look at wave sailing in more detail later in this chapter.

掌舵：这时候，船是无法正顺航行的。如果航行不是特别稳定的话，可以稍微迎风一些，让气流穿过帆或将帆调到与风同舷的位置。风大时很可能会起浪，要好好控舵、注意抓浪。我们会在本章的后续内容中就应对波浪进行更详细的阐述。

Body movement: Move back in the boat as the wind increases. Ensure the bow doesn't dig in.

身体动作：随着风力上升，移回到船内。防止船头下沉。

Once you are planing, sail the boat flat rather than kited. In semi-planing conditions, get the boat dead flat and watch out for gusts. Sail a little high in the lulls. Just as a gust is about to strike, give a pump (one per gust) and slide back in the boat in one smooth strong movement—you are away! Keep the boat level at all costs but immediately release the sheet back out so the sail is at maximum power. Trim the boat fore and aft to keep the bow just up and planing.

一旦开始滑行，就要保持船体水平，而不是反压舷。在半滑行状态，务必使船体完全水平，注意阵风。在风间歇时，角度更迎风一些。在即将通过阵风时，收放主缭鼓动船帆（每次阵风），回到船内——你就要开始滑浪了！操作要一气呵成，坚定流畅。尽全力保持船体水平，但要迅速将主缭松出去，使船帆充分受风，达到最大帆力。前后调节船体，使船头保持刚好抬起，持续滑行。

> **DID YOU KNOW? 你知道吗？**
>
> Rule 42.3c allows you to pump the sail once to initiate surfing or planing for each gust or wave. Once you are planing you're not allowed to pump.
>
> 规则 42.3c 允许你在每次遇到阵风或浪的时候，摇帆一次，使船开始冲浪或滑行。一旦开始滑行，就不允许再摇帆。

Downwind Wave Sailing
顺风滑浪

This is the pure essence of sailing! The pain of beating stops and magic happens. The aim is to keep sliding down the fronts or sailing the tops of the waves for as long as possible. On the front face of a wave you have clear strong wind, can slide downhill, and have the water movement with you. That's your target area. Troughs are bad news because you lose the wind and the water movement slows you down.

这绝对是帆船的精髓！艰苦的迎风段结束了，接下来就是见证奇迹的时刻了。顺风滑浪的操作目标是，保持从浪前滑下来，或尽可能保持在浪尖。在浪前，你的受风会更强、更清晰，能够顺着浪往下滑，而且水的移动也会有助于航行。你的目标就是保持在浪前。落到浪谷的位置就不妙了，不仅受风不好，而且水的移动还会使你减速。

Catching Waves 抓浪

So, you're out on a perfectly honking day with a big swell rolling in. Taking a wave is like jumping onto a moving train. You've got to run fast before you jump, so head up and sheet in as your ride approaches and pump once if you get a gust to initiate planing.

假设在某一个航行日出航，风况"完美"，波涛汹涌，巨浪滚滚，非常适合练习滑浪。抓浪就像要跳上一辆移动的火车。你必须在滑浪之前，让船有很好的速度。所以在靠近浪时，要迎风偏转，收帆加速。在遇到阵风时，就收主缭一次，使船开始滑浪。

As the wave starts to lift the back of the boat, bear off hard down the wave, hike out and back, and watch out for the death roll. Feel the acceleration. The boat's got to get up to the speed of the wave or be left behind, so now lean forward to dip the nose and increase sliding. Give a hearty pump, balanced by hiking out or back, and the boat will shoot forward again, accelerating to the wave's speed and slipping down the face of the wave.

随着浪开始将船尾抬起，顺风偏转下浪，坐到船外压舷，并向后移动，注意避免正顺翻覆。感受船的加速。船速必须达到浪的速度，否则就会追不上浪。所以，这种时候，身体要往前倾，使船头下沉，使船下滑更快。大力收放主缭，鼓动船帆，坐到船外或船后，调节船的左右平衡，船就会再次往前加速，加速到与浪同速，从浪前往下滑行。

Staying On The Wave 保持与浪同步

If you shoot at full speed straight down a steep face, you will overtake the wave, reach the trough, and possibly nose-dive filling the boat with water or even pitchpole. At the very least you will slow down in the trough, having run out of wind and slope, and the wave will rush past and leave you behind. To prevent this, head up and sail along the wave or bear away and sail by the lee sailing along the wave the other way.

如果你顺着陡峭的浪，在浪前全速滑行，你就会超过浪的速度，滑到浪谷，这可能会使船头扎进水里，导致船进水，甚至使船往船头翻覆。至少在浪谷，你的速度会减慢，既没有风，也没有斜坡的推动，浪会迅速往前掠过你，将你甩在后面。为了防止这种情况发生，你可

Catching a wave 抓浪

Spot a wave you can catch
观察水面，确定要抓的浪

Head up to increase speed
迎风偏转，提高船速

Then bear away down the wave
顺风偏转下浪

And pump the main
收放主缭，鼓动主帆

Move your weight forward
身体前移

Then back to avoid a nose-dive
然后往后移动，避免船头扎水

Sail diagonally along the wave
沿着浪斜向航行

Surf the wave for as long as possible
尽可能保持滑浪

Just before you drop off the wave, head up to maintain speed for the next wave
在你即将完成一个滑浪时，迎风偏转，保持船速，迎接下一个浪

以迎风偏转，随浪航行，或顺风偏转，使帆与风同舷（反帆），在另一个方向顺浪航行。

This takes a lot of practice to do well. This is what a lot of people call up turns and down turns.

这个技巧需要花很多时间练习才能掌握。这就是大多数人所说的迎偏和顺偏滑浪。

The Down Turn 顺偏滑浪
- Heel the boat over on top of you
- 使船体往你这边倾斜
- Sharply drop the main to 90° or maybe a bit further
- 快速将主帆松至 90° 或者更远的位置
- Let the rudder steer away as the heel wants to turn the boat
- 操控船舵使船往下风转，因为船的倾斜会使其偏转
- Balance the boat so you ride the wave diagonally down
- 平衡船体，斜着在浪上滑行
- Be careful not to death roll: this takes practice
- 小心航行，避免正顺翻覆：一定要有耐心

The Up Turn 迎偏滑浪
- Heel the boat slightly away from you so the boat wants to head up
- 稍微使船往你的对侧倾斜，使船迎风偏转
- Sheet the main in slightly
- 稍微收紧主帆
- Let the rudder steer the boat up
- 操控船舵使船往上风转
- Balance the boat so you ride the wave diagonally up
- 平衡船体，斜着在浪上滑行

Dropping Off 掉浪

At some point you will fall off the wave. The answer is to realize that you are falling off the wave early and point up to keep your speed, sail high and fast along the back of the wave and in the trough, and finally bear off on the face of the next wave. In irregular waves it's necessary to watch their development like a hawk to grab a ride.

在某个时刻，你会从浪上掉下来。解决方法是，尽快意识到你在下降，然后迎风偏转，保持船速。在浪背和浪谷时高角度快速航行，最后，在来到下一个浪的浪前时才顺风偏转。在无规律的浪中航行，要像老鹰一样密切观察浪的起伏，看准时机，抓浪滑行。

You want to be sailing down the wave
尽量下浪航行

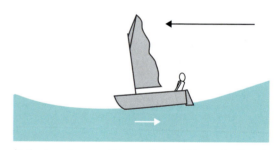

In the trough you will lose wind and the water flow is against you
在浪谷时，无风且水流与你的航行方向相反

Downwind sailing in waves is always different. Waves vary in size, length, angle and speed. All of these variations require slightly different styles of the above techniques. Sometimes it is easy to catch waves running by the lee, other times up turns work well due to the wave angle or sometimes just straight down the face of the wave is best when the wave is moving very fast.

在波浪中顺风航行的情景总是不同的。浪的大小、长度、角度和速度富于变化。这就需要水手们在应用上述技巧时，稍微做出一些调整。有时，在帆与风同舷（反帆），顺风航行时很容易抓浪；而其他时候，由于浪的角度，往上偏转则更好用一些；或者有时在浪移动非常快速时，顺着浪直接滑下来最好。

Practice makes perfect! You must sail downwind in waves until your response to the characteristics of each wave becomes automatic, freeing you to ride them in the most effective manner.

熟能生巧！你必须不断练习在波浪中顺风航行，直到你能够本能地应对每一种浪，从而以最高效的方式随心所欲地驾驭浪。

Sailing By The Lee
帆与风同舷

While sailing by the lee is useful when staying on a wave, it is also a valuable skill worth working on. It gives the advantages of:

要保持与浪步调一致，帆与风同舷（反帆）航行非常有效，而且这一技巧非常值得学习。它能带来各种优势：

- Freedom to manoeuvre, and more options on the run
- 操作自由，顺风航行时有更多选择
- Better chance of getting the inside position at the leeward mark
- 在绕下风标时，有更多的机会来到浮标内侧
- Starboard tack advantages for the whole run
- 整个顺风航段都有右舷的优势
- The option to bear off, away from covering boats
- 能够顺风偏转，远离遮盖船
- The ability to bear away to break overlaps
- 能够进行顺风偏转，打破相联
- Freedom to ride wave faces in either direction
- 随心所欲地驾驭各个方向的浪
- Potentially quicker than dead downwind as the wind attaches easily over the leech and the flow across the sail generates more power
- 可能比正顺航行更快，因为风可以轻松流畅地吹过帆后缘，气流穿过帆面，产生更多动力

Begin to practise sailing by the lee in the light winds and do not try to kite. Bear away, holding the tiller extension at the universal joint and crouching in the boat, leaning inboard. Let the sheet out progressively, keep bearing away until you are reaching along with the boom forward of the mast and the wind crossing the sail from leech to luff. You can check this by looking at the telltails. Bearing away now makes the boat actually come up into the wind and eases the sail, while heading up fills the sail with wind, heeling the boat more.

刚开始练习在小风中反帆航行时，先不要尝试反压帆。顺风偏转，抓住副舵柄万向节处控舵，蹲在船内，身体往里倾。逐渐松主缭，一直顺偏到侧顺风航行，横杆比桅杆更靠前，风从帆后缘吹往帆前缘。你可以观察并检查气流。这时候顺风偏转，实际上会使船从另一舷更加迎风，松帆，迎风偏转，使帆完全受风，使船倾斜更多。

Enjoy this for a bit, then try bearing away more until the bottom of the leech starts to flick: you are near to the gybing point. Either luff a little or ease the sheet to fill the sail. Fun! To get back to a normal run again, luff up slowly and pull in the mainsheet as you do it. Well done!

稍微适应这种操作后，试着顺风偏转更多，直到帆后缘的底部开始抖动：即将顺风转向时，可以迎风偏转一点或松点主缭，使帆受风。这很有意思吧！要回到正常的顺风航行，就缓慢地迎风偏转，同时收主缭。做得好！

When racing you would not sail so low—keep the boom at 90° to the centreline (less in strong winds). Bear away to reverse the flow on the telltails. Now try to keep the boat sailing as straight downwind as possible with the telltails still reversed.

在比赛时，不要这样低角度航行——保持横杆与船的中心线成90°（在强风中的角度小一些）。顺风偏转，使气流线上的气流反向通过。然后，试着让船尽可能地保持正顺航行，气流线依旧反向。

In strong winds get your feet more into the middle, with the tiller extension on the leeward gunwale and your body leaning to leeward and facing forward. Everything works backwards!

Stabilise the boat in the gusts by bearing away more and / or by pulling in the sheet. In the lulls power up by doing the opposite! In smooth water it's possible to kite by the lee.

在强风中，把双脚置于更靠近中间的位置，副舵柄置于下风船舷，身体往下风倾斜，面朝前方。操作顺序倒过来也是一样的！为了在阵风中平衡船体，顺风偏转更多并且/或者收紧主缭。如果想在弱风中提高动力，就做相反的操作！在平缓的水面上，可以在帆与风同舷时反压舷。

Running by the lee
在侧顺反帆角度航行

Reaching
横风航行

Beam Reach / Close Reach 横风 / 后迎风

Many of the techniques used for running are applicable to reaching.
很多顺风航行的技巧均适用于横风航行。

Boat set-up: Trim the sail carefully to the telltails. You are sailing the boat in the direction you want to go, so any change in wind strength or direction needs to be matched by playing your mainsheet and keeping the telltails flying.
船只设置： 观察气流线，小心地调节船帆。在驶向目标方向时，如有任何风力或风向的改变，都需要相应地调节主缭，保持气流线飘起。

On a reach in medium wind you often need more kicking strap (vang) than you require on a run to keep the head of the sail driving as well as the base. The kicker is difficult to adjust but, if the reach is long, it may be worth trying to pull it on. To do this, sheet the main in hard as quickly as you can and pull the kicker tight then release the main.

中等风力中横风航行，为了保持帆顶和帆底边的驱动力，相比顺风航行，你通常需要更多地收紧斜拉器。调节斜拉器比较困难，但是如果横风段较长，还是值得尝试收紧斜拉器的。为此，以最快的速度收紧主帆，收紧斜拉器，然后松主帆。

Steering: Spot the mark and try to sail a

straight line to it. However, if it is gusty, it may pay to come up in the lulls and bear away in the gusts to keep the best speed.

掌舵：确定目的浮标，试着直线航行抵达浮标。不过，如果有阵风的话，有利的做法是，在弱风中迎风偏转，在阵风中顺风偏转，以保持最佳船速。

Body movement: The boat must be kept flat so there is no weather helm. Concentrate on boat trim as you would on the upwind. In the gusts try moving back to get the boat planing and remember: one pump per gust to initiate a plane.

肢体动作：必须保持船体水平，以避免上风舵。和迎风航行时一样，专注于调节船的前后平衡。在阵风中时，试着往船后移动，使船进入滑行状态，同时，记住：每次遇到阵风就摇帆一次，使船开始滑行。

Broad Reach 侧顺风航行

As you get broader, all the techniques become more like a run. But remember to pay particular attention to your telltails and try to keep them flying. This is where all the power comes from.

航行角度越大，操作技巧越贴近顺风航行。但要记得重点关注气流线，使其尽量保持飘起的状态，以获得持续的动力。

Optimist sailing on a close reach with the helm keeping the boat flat
驾驶 OP 后迎风航行，舵手正在努力地保持船的水平

Optimist sailing on a broad reach with the helm concentrating on the telltales
驾驶 OP 侧顺风航行，舵手正在认真观察气流线

BOAT HANDLING & TACTICS
操控与技术

PART 2 第二部分

CHAPTER 5 第五章
Basic Boat Handing 基本控船

Great boat handling is a vital requirement for top level Optimist sailing. Not only does it get you around the course quicker—it also gives you confidence that you can perform in tight situations, giving you more options for overtaking.

要具备顶级的 OP 航行技术，出色的控船技术必不可少。出色的控船不仅能够让你更快地完成航线——而且，也会让你更有信心在紧张的情况下充分展示自己的技术，并且为你提供更多超船的选择。

Tacking
迎风转向

The Roll Tack 滚动迎风转向

Boatspeed may be maintained through a tack by roll tacking. Here's how to do it:

运用滚动迎风转向保持船速。具体操作步骤如下：

- When you decide to tack, bear away a little and heel the boat to leeward.
- 在决定要迎风转向后，顺风偏转一点，使船倾向下风。
- Then smoothly roll the boat right over to windward as you steer through the wind squeezing the mainsail in as you do.
- 然后流畅地往上风侧滚动船体，同时，推舵穿过风，收紧主帆。
- By the time the hull is pointing on the new close-hauled course, the gunwale will be touching the water and the boom should have come over your head onto the new side. Your feet should be under you, placed on the inside of the chine between the boat's bottom and side.
- 随着船转到另一舷迎风航向，船舷会触到水面，横杆应从你头顶转过，来到另一侧。应将双脚置于身体下方，位于舭缘线（船底边）内侧，在船底和船侧之间。
- Stand up, bear off a little more so that the boat is just below the new close-hauled course, ease the mainsail a little and place your back foot across the boat to the inside of the windward chine.
- 站起来，再顺风偏转一点，使船刚好转到另一侧迎风角度靠下一点的位置，松一点主帆，后脚跨过船只，来到上风侧舭缘线内侧。
- Smoothly and carefully transfer your weight from one foot to the other, rolling the boat upright to her new beating trim. Squeeze the mainsail in as you do.
- 小心流畅地将你的身体重心换到另一只脚上，滚动船体至水平，转到另一侧迎风航行进行调节，同时收紧主帆。
- Cross the boat and sit on the new windward gunwale. Do not let go of the tiller extension, but steer with your arm holding the tiller extension behind your back.
- 跨过船另一侧，坐到上风船舷上。不要松掉副舵柄，用手臂夹住副舵柄，将其置于背后控舵。
- Only when the boat is sailing well on the new tack should you change your hands around and take the tiller extension in your back hand.
- 只有当船在新的一舷航行良好时，你才应该换手，用后手拿副舵柄。

When practising tacking, try counting yourself through the movements. Then try tacking as slowly as you can to the same count

CHAPTER 5 第五章 | **Basic Boat Handing 基本控船**

sequence. Next, try fast counting and tacking. Through experimenting you will find a particular rate of tacking will feel fast and comfortable.

在练习迎风转向时，数一数自己的操作步骤。然后，按照同样的顺序，试着以最慢的速度再次转向。之后，试着在转向时，加快操作和数步骤的速度。在多次实践后，你会找到一个最快最舒服的迎风转向速度。

Keep practising until you tack perfectly without needing to count or even think about what you are doing.

不断练习，直到你能够完美地进行迎风转向，不需要数步骤，甚至不需要思考你在做什么。

Don't tack on impulse. When a tack is needed keep driving, check for right-of-way boats, and look ahead for a flat patch. Tack on the top of a wave in one movement.

不要冲动地进行迎风转向。在需要转向时，保持航行，注意观察有航行权的船只，并寻找前方平坦的水域。在浪尖上迎风转向则要一气呵成。

Timing and speed of movement change as a sailor gets bigger. Be careful to re-look at your tack as you grow. Some sailors have an awesome roll tack when they are young but, as they grow, they don't adapt the tack and it starts to look clumsy.

Sailing close-hauled
迎风角度航行

Begin to steer into the wind
开始推舵转向迎风

Continue the turn
继续转动

Roll the boat as the boom centres and squeeze the mainsail
在横杆居中时，滚动船体，收紧主帆

Ease the main as the boom comes over your head and prepare to move to the other side
随着横杆转到头顶，松主帆，准备移动到船的另一侧

Bring the boat upright
将船压到水平

OPTIMIST RACING OP 级帆船竞赛

Sitting on the new gunwale
坐到船的另一舷

Swap hands once established on the new tack and concentrate on the telltails
一旦在新的一侧稳定下来，就换手，专注于观察气流线

And get up to maximum speed on the new tack
在新的一侧以最快速度航行

　　随着水手的块头变大，操作的时间和速度也会改变。所以，在成长过程中，要注意反观自己迎风转向的技巧。有的水手在年轻的时候能够非常出色地进行滚动迎风转向，但是随着他们逐渐长大，没有相应地调节自己的转向技巧，动作逐渐显得笨拙。

The Max-Power Tack 最大动力迎风转向

　　Once you are overpowered going upwind you should change your style of tacking. There is no need to roll tack since you haven't the weight to pull it down as you come out the tack.

　　一旦迎风航行时受风过大，你就应该改变迎风转向的方式。如果你的体重不够，就没有必要进行滚动迎风转向，因为你无法在转向后将船体压下来。

　　Now the priority is to come out of the tack as flat as possible. Practise crossing the boat slightly earlier and jumping straight into your hiking position. Then you can power up the boat and accelerate away.

　　现在的首要任务是，在转向后，使船尽可能地保持平稳。练习稍早一些穿过船体，直接跨到压舷的位置上。然后，提高航行动力，加速驶离。

Begin the turn
开始转向

Heading into the wind
转到顶风

So the boom centres
横杆居中

CHAPTER 5 第五章 | Basic Boat Handing 基本控船

Duck under the boom
压低身体至横杆之下

And begin to cross the boat
然后开始穿过船体

As the sail fills move quickly to the new side
随着帆受风，快速移动到另一侧

Sit down on the new side
坐到新的一侧

Establishing yourself on the new tack
在新的一侧稳定下来

Before swapping hands
在换手之前

Double Tacking 两个连续的迎风转向

Double tacking whilst stationary is an essential skill for Optimist sailors in the minutes before the start. While beating very slowly on starboard, tack onto port, sail for a boat length, and then tack back to starboard and stop. The entire double tack must be achieved as quickly as possible to avoid the risk of impeding a starboard tack boat. The initial tack from being stationary on starboard to port is achieved by rolling well to windward for acceleration, and then pulling the boom across to increase spin. The boat must be kept heeled right over until it points below the port close-hauled course. Then roll the boat upright, getting maximum drive from the sail.

在起航前几分钟，从静止状态连续两次迎风转向（迎风双转）是 OP 水手的一项基本技能。在迎风段，非常缓慢地右舷航行，先迎风转向到左舷，航行一倍船长的距离，然后转回到右舷航行并停船。两次迎风转向的操作越快越好，以免阻碍其他右舷船。从右舷静止状态，迎风转向到左舷的操作方法是：向上风侧滚动船体进行加速，然后将横杆拉到另一侧，使船继续旋转。保持船只倾斜，直到船在左舷航行低于迎风角度，然后将船压平，使帆受风最大。

After sailing as close as you can to the boats to windward (shouting "Hold your course"[①]), roll

---

① 原版图书此处即为双引号。

tack back onto starboard and stop the boat by holding the boom amidships for a few seconds as you step across. You are now in the enviable position of having a beautiful gap under you to power off into at the starting signal!

在尽可能靠近你上风侧的船只时（大喊"保持你的航向"），滚动迎风转向回到右舷，在跨到船另一侧时，抓住横杆，使其在船中间停留几秒，从而使船停下来。这样，你就处在一个十分令人羡慕的位置了，你为下风侧创造了非常好的空隙，可以在起航信号发出时随时加速起航！

To create a gap
为了制造更多空隙

Boat 122 tacks off
帆号122的船只迎风转向驶离

Onto port
转到左舷航行

And tacks back
然后迎风转向回来

With a gap
这样就有了空隙

To power into at the starting signal
在起航信号发出时，加速进入起航线

PRACTICE IDEAS 练习方法

Tacking & Double-Tacking Practice
迎风转向 & 连续双迎风转向练习

There are lots of ways you can practise tacking.

迎风转向的练习方式有很多。

On your own you can just go out and do lots of tacks up a short beat. This could be a mix of single and double tacks.

如果你独自在水上训练的话，可以设置一个短迎风航线，进行多次迎风转向练习。可以结合单次转向和连续双迎风转向练习。

But with a coach, this can be made more interesting because you don't necessarily decide when to tack and there are other boats involved which makes things tighter and more competitive.

但是，如果有一名教练一起的话，可以进行更有趣的练习，因为你不必决定什么时候迎风转向。而且，如果有其他船只参与，训练会更加紧凑，更有竞争性。

1. Tacking on the whistle: Start with the sailors well-spaced out on the same tack. All sailors tack when the coach blows the whistle. For variety, this exercise can be done with eyes shut!

哨令迎风转向：开始时，让水手们同舷航行，均匀地分布在起航线上。随着教练的哨声响起，水手们全部迎风转向。为使训练更多样化，可以让他们闭着眼睛操作！

It is easy to see who is tacking better because everyone tacks at the same time and so the sailors who make the most gains are the best at tacking!

这样，就很容易看出谁的迎风转向更好，因为每个人都同时操作，所以航行最远的水手迎风转向技术最强！

2. Tacking in the triangle: Set a short start line and a short beat with a windward mark. Play it as a normal practice race but there is one additional rule—you cannot sail outside the triangle formed by the start line and windward mark. This means that, as you sail upwind, the triangle gets smaller and you have to tack more often.

迎风转向三角标：起航线设置要短，距离上风标近些，保证迎风航段较短。大体和平时的练习赛一样，除了增加一条规则——不允许在起航线和上风标形成的三角区外航行。这就意味着，随着水手们往上迎风航行，三角区会越来越小，那么水手们就需要更频繁地转向。

It also gets tighter with other boats at the top of the triangle, really testing the boat handling.

而且，在三角区顶部，和其他船也会更加贴近，十分考验水手们的控船能力。

3. Double tacking up the line: Set a start line and the boats all line up near the pin end. The windward boat does a double tack to create more space to leeward. As soon as they have lined up again, the next boat does a double tack, and so on until everyone is lined up at the other end of the line.

起航线连续双迎风转向：设置一条起航线，让所有的船从左端起排成一条线停在起航线上。上风船连续两次迎风转向，为下风制造更多空隙。一旦所有的船再次排成一条线，下一条船就进行连续双迎风转向，一直往下进行，直到所有人在起航线的另一端排成一条直线。

Gybing
顺风转向

Light Wind Gybe 小风顺风转向

Gybing can be tricky, and you must practise until it becomes automatic:

顺风转向并不简单，你必须不断练习，直到形成肌肉记忆：

- Check that the daggerboard will not foul the boom or strop.
- 检查并确保稳向板不会挡住横杆或三角绳。
- Pull in approximately 50cm of mainsheet, keep the boat level or heeled a little to windward, and bear away smoothly.
- 主缭收紧约 50 cm，保持船体水平，或者略微往上风侧倾斜，然后流畅地顺风偏转。
- Lean in and grasp all three parts of the mainsheet about 50cm above the lower blocks but keep the tail of the mainsheet in your same hand. (This is easier than it sounds.) As the weight comes off the sheet, pull the boom across.
- 身体往里倾斜，抓住下滑轮上方约 50 cm 的主缭绳圈，但是保持同一只手抓住主缭末端（听起来复杂，做起来容易）。随着主缭上的受力减小，将横杆拉到另一侧。
- Let the boat roll until the boom almost hits the water.
- 滚动船体，直到横杆几乎碰到水面。
- Then simultaneously:
- 同时：
  - As the boom flies across, let go of the three parts of the mainsheet but keep the tail, ease the sheet a small amount to absorb some of the force.
  - 随着横杆晃过，松掉主缭绳圈，但要继续抓住末端，松一点主缭，减少帆的受力。
  - Step across the boat and sit on the new windward side—well aft.
  - 跨到船另一侧坐下来——尽量靠船尾。
  - Move the tiller back to the mid-line to keep the boat sailing straight until total control is regained—you will be steering with the extension behind your back.
  - 舵柄居中，保持直线行驶，直到航行平稳——这期间你需要在背后用副舵柄控船。
- Swap hands like you would in a tack.
- 最后，换手，像迎风转向一样。

Lower the daggerboard
放下稳向板

Sheet in a handful of the main
收一把主缭

Start to turn
开始转向

CHAPTER 5 第五章 | **Basic Boat Handing 基本控船**

Steer around and grab the mainsheet falls
转舵，抓住主缭绳圈

Pull the boom over
将横杆拉过来

Letting the boat roll
滚动船体

Move to the new side and pull the boat upright
移动到另一侧，将船压平

Steer and balance the boat
控好舵并平衡船体

Swap hands and pull the daggerboard up
换手，拉起稳向板

Heavy Wind Gybe 大风顺风转向

In a windier gybe it can be quite scary. But don't let the boat take control of you. Be positive and definite about a windy gybe.

在大风中顺风转向可能会很吓人，但是不要让船失去控制。对此要保持积极和相信的态度。

- Make sure you are going fast: as fast as you can before you start your gybe.
- 确保高速航行：在开始顺风转向前，越快越好。
- Try to pick a good time to gybe—going down a wave, in a flat patch or in a lull.
- 选择一个好的时机顺风转向——下浪时，水域平坦或是风间歇的时候。
- Don't roll the boat so much.
- 不要过多地滚动船体。
- The key to surviving is accurate steering of the boat. An 'S' works best, so steer up to gain speed, turn through the gybe then bear away to balance the boat.
- 顺利完成的关键是精准地控舵。"S"形航线效果最佳，往上偏转提高船速，然后顺转向，再顺风偏转，平衡船体。

57

OPTIMIST RACING OP级帆船竞赛

Grab the mainsheet falls
抓住主缭绳圈

Pull the boom over
将横杆拉到另一侧

So it crosses the centreline
随着横杆来到中心线

Get up to the new side
起身来到另一侧

To balance the boat
压舷

And get it upright and bear away to turn back
将船压平，然后顺风偏转使船更顺风一些

Balance the boat
平衡船体

Swap hands
换手

Look for the next gust or wave to catch
注意观察，准备抓下一个阵风或浪

CHAPTER 5 第五章   Basic Boat Handing 基本控船

Gybing Mistakes 顺风转向错误

Tripping over the daggerboard: If you turn a sharp corner at speed with the daggerboard too far down, the boat slips sideways while the daggerboard grips the water. The result is a roll to leeward as a minimum and sometimes even a capsize.

稳向板受阻： 如果你在稳向板过低的情况下快速急转，稳向板就会被水绊住，使船侧移。其结果最轻的是，船滚向下风，严重的时候甚至会导致翻覆。

To avoid this, have the daggerboard at 30cm height. Any higher than this and it will hit the boom as it comes over. You can draw a line on the board so you know the correct position.

为了避免这种情况，稳向板的高度应设置为30 cm。如果高于此高度，就会在横杆转动的时候发生碰撞。你可以在板上画一条线作为记号，以便掌握正确的位置。

Broaching: Loss of control just before the boom comes over, followed by the boat screwing back onto her previous course, is due either to the boat heeling to leeward (the leeward chine digs in and steers her back up into the wind), or having the sail too far out making it harder to pull over to gybe.

打横： 在横杆转到另一侧前，控制不够，导致船转回原来的方向。要么是因为船倾向下风（下风侧船底边扎进水里，使船转回迎风），要么就是帆松出去过多，很难使横杆换到另一舷，进行顺风转向。

Think about your timing of pulling the mainsheet over and the steering of the boat. These need to be coordinated.

考虑好收主缭和拉舵的时机，两者应相互协调。

Nose-diving: Nose-diving is usually caused by too much water in the boat and / or the helm not sitting far enough back. Done with style this can result in the boat rolling transom over bow, with the helm landing on the sail or even in the water ahead.

船头扎水： 通常是由于船内积水过多引起的，并且/或者舵手坐得不够靠后。严重的话，可能会导致船尾翻向船头，舵手被甩到帆上，甚至是船前方的水中。

Bail regularly to ensure the minimum amount of water in the boat and sit further back.

水手应经常排水，确保船内少有积水，坐的位置尽量靠后。

Bear Away
顺风偏转

A good bear away can give you a great tactical advantage for the next leg. The key is to make the turn fast and smooth and to try not to use the rudder as a brake.

良好的顺风偏转会让你在下一个航段取得很大的战术优势。操作关键是快且流畅地转向，尽量不要用舵，过多使用会使其更像一个类似刹车的制动装置。

- As you approach the mark, make sure that your mainsheet has no tangles in it. Hold it above your head with your mainsheet hand so it can be released easily.
- 随着你逐渐靠近浮标，检查确保主缭无缠结。将其置于头顶，以便松缭。
- As you round the mark, start the bear away by releasing the mainsheet. Lead with the mainsail, not the rudder, and don't sit in.
- 绕标后开始松主缭，进行顺风偏转。运用主帆而并非舵来主导操作，不要坐到船内。
- The boat will heel on top of you and want to bear away. Let the rudder follow where the boat wants to go.
- 船会往你上方倾斜，往顺风偏转。让舵跟随船的航行。
- Control the speed of the turn with the heel of the boat. Move in and flatten the boat to stop the turn.
- 倾斜船体，以控制转向速度。身体移到船内，压平船体，停止转向。
- Don't forget to pull your daggerboard up and check your settings once you are going in the right direction.
- 一旦你进入正确的航向，别忘了提起稳向板，检查各项设置。

OPTIMIST RACING OP 级帆船竞赛

To bear away, from hiking on the beat
从迎风压舷的位置开始进行顺风偏转

Begin to bear away, releasing the mainsheet
开始松主缭，进行顺风偏转

Heeling the boat to windward to help the turn
使船倾向上风，辅助转向

As you continue to bear away
继续顺风偏转

Onto the new leg
转到新航段

And raise the daggerboard
然后提起稳向板

Head Up
迎风偏转

Rounding up onto the beat can be a very important part of the race. Holding a lane and keeping out of dirty air after the mark can give you a lot more tactical options.

绕标后的迎风航段在比赛中非常关键。在绕完标后，保持最佳迎风角度和清晰的受风会让你有更多战术选择。

- Push your daggerboard down early. It only slows the boat marginally and you don't want to be rushing as you need to make the rounding.
- 早些放下稳向板。这只会轻微减慢船速，而且不会让你在绕标时手忙脚乱。
- Heel the boat to leeward to make it head up. Try to make a smooth turn coming in wide and leaving the mark tight so you are not in anyone's dirty air and will have an option to tack at the start of the beat.
- 将船倾向下风，迎风偏转。试着流畅地偏转，以大角度靠近浮标，贴标驶离（宽进窄出），避免被其他船只影响受风，而且你也能选择在迎风航段开始时，进行迎风转向。
- As you turn, pull the mainsheet in hand-over-

hand matching the speed of the turn.
- 在偏转时，用双手连续收主缭，配合偏转的速度。
- Once around the mark, concentrate on the telltails and speed. Check your sail to make sure it is set right.
- 一旦绕完标，就专注于运用气流线调节船速。检查船帆，确保设置正确。

Heading up 迎风偏转

As you prepare to head up, lower the daggerboard
在准备迎风偏转时，放下稳向板

Sail to the buoy
驶向浮标

Round up as you reach the buoy
到达浮标后进行绕标

Pull in the mainsheet to match your turn
收紧主缭，配合偏转速度

Pulling in hand-over-hand
双手连续收缭

And hike
然后压舷

OPTIMIST RACING OP 级帆船竞赛

Other Boat Handling
其他控船技术

Stopping 停船

You need to be able to stop during pre-start manoeuvres, to avoid pile-ups at marks and going for the inside position, or when team racing, which can often become 'Go Slow' racing.

在起航准备阶段，你要能够使船停下来，避免和其他船一起挤在标旁，并抢占内侧的位置。在团体赛中也需要停船，因为团体赛通常会演变成一场"慢速"比赛。

To slow down or stop:
减速或停船方式：

- Weave about from side to side, using the rudder more than necessary
- 左右摇晃船只，更多地使用舵
- Ease the sail or pull the sail in if running
- 在顺风航行时，过度松帆或者收帆
- Sit out over the stern and sink the transom—this increases drag enormously
- 坐到船尾板外侧，使尾板下沉——大大增加航行阻力
- Luff with the sail eased
- 松帆迎风偏转
- Push the boom out if going upwind
- 迎风航行时，将横杆推出

To stop, luff, ease the sail right out and sit over the transom to sink the stern
停船操作：迎风偏转，将帆完全松出，坐到船尾板上，使船尾下沉

Accelerating 加速

Accelerating or triggering is a vital skill to help you get away from the start line cleanly. You must have space below you at the start, having made a slow controlled approach.

加速或起速是顺利起航的关键技能。在靠近起航线时，放慢速度，控好船，务必在下方留有空间。

Just before the starting signal, from stationary:
在起航信号正要发出前，你还是静止状态：

- Heel the boat away and head just off close-hauled with the sail just pulling.
- 使船体倾斜，迎风偏转到稍微低于迎风角度，帆刚好开始受风。
- Roll the boat upright and head up.

To stop quicker, push the boom into the wind
为了更快停船，将横杆往顶风推出去

- 将船压平,继续迎风偏转。
- Adjust the boat's heading (with the rudder) onto the perfect close-hauled course and, at the same time, sheet in the mainsail to the beating position just over the corner of the transom, but do not over-sheet.
- 调节航向(用舵完成),使船在最佳迎风角度上航行,同时收紧主帆,使后帆角刚好在帆尾板的角的上方,为迎风航段做准备。
- 注意不要过度收帆。
- Check your heel and fore-and-aft trim. Don't hit a wave!
- 检查倾斜角度,调节船的前后平衡。千万不要撞浪!
- Apply maximum hiking power if the wind requires it and concentrate on the telltails.
- 如果风力过大,应最大程度地压舷,注意观察气流线。

Accelerating off the line 起航线加速

To accelerate off the start, bear away slightly
为了加速冲出起航线,先稍微顺风偏转

Heel the boat to leeward
使船倾向下风

Pull it upright and the mainsail in
压平船体,收主帆

And concentrate on the telltails
认真观察气流线并进行调节

PRACTICE IDEAS 练习方法

Sailing Backwards 倒退航行

This is worth trying now and again, for fun and as practice for getting out of irons. It is an essential skill for confident manoeuvring at the start when you often need to move back as well as forward under full control, especially if you need to re-position on the start line.

此练习非常值得一试，不仅充满乐趣，还能帮助你练习驶出顶风区。这一技巧对培养水手们起航自信十分关键，因为很多时候大家都需要能完全控制船只的进退，尤其是在起航线上重新寻找空位时。

- Luff and get into irons.
- 迎风偏转，进入顶风区。
- Try to steer downwind without touching the sail, going backwards on starboard tack. The stern goes in the direction the tiller points.
- 试着在顺风航行时不碰帆，右舷倒退航行。舵柄的指向即为船倒退的方向。
- Get out of irons and get sailing as quickly as possible on starboard tack.
- 驶出顶风，尽快开始右舷航行。
- When getting out of irons, lifting the daggerboard will help more than pulling or pushing the sail.
- 在驶出顶风区后，抬起稳向板比拉推主帆更有帮助。
- If you want to go backwards faster, when head to wind, hold the boom to windward.
- 如果你想更快速地倒退航行，就在船顶风时，将横杆推向上风侧。

Push the boom out into the wind
将横杆推向迎风

Steer the boat in reverse
反向控舵

Until you can establish yourself on the new tack
直到你在新的一舷稳定航行

CHAPTER 6 第六章
Tactics 战 术

Tactics is a huge subject. You should read *Tactics to Win* by Nick Craig or *Tactics Made Simple* by Jon Emmett, both also part of Fernhurst Books' Sail to Win series, which cover all the situations that crop up on the race course. In this chapter we'll look at the most important parts of the course.

战术是一个非常大的主题。应该好好读一读尼克·克雷格的《战术制胜》和乔恩·埃米特的《极简战术》，两本书均为Fernhurst"航向胜利"系列书籍中的作品，书中涵盖了在帆船比赛中出现的各种场景。在本章中，我们会讨论比赛中最重要的部分。

The Start
起航

Start priorities are:
起航首要任务：
- To get a 'front line' start.
- 在船群第一排起航。
- To have a gap to leeward for acceleration.
- 制造下风空当，以便加速。
- To start at the right end of the line.
- 从起航线正确的一端起航。
- Be active! Be dynamic! Be pushy! Be dominant!
- 积极主动！精神饱满！强势进取！保持主导！
- Don't hit people. Stay legal.
- 不要撞船，遵守规则。

Starting lines in Optimist races are very congested, and a remarkable amount of boat contact, sail contact and dubious practice take place. You will survive if you keep awake with both eyes open. Shout in good time if you think somebody will foul you in any way.

OP帆船比赛的起航线会十分拥挤，不仅有大量的船体接触和船帆接触，而且各种令人疑惑的情况也很常见。保持警觉，睁大双眼，你就能争得一席之地。如有任何可能的犯规行为阻碍你的航行，应及时大声呼喊。

Picking Where To Start 选择起航位置

Have a good routine before the start:
在起航前，确保有一个良好的操作流程：
- Sail upwind and feel what is a lift and what is a header. How much and how often is it shifting? Is there a reason why one side of the beat might pay? If there is, check it out by doing a split tack with your buddy.
- 迎风航行一段，感受风摆是上升还是下降。变化幅度是多少？摆动频率如何？迎风航段的某一侧是不是更有利一些？为什么？如果有优势差异，和你的练习伙伴分别从左右舷进行迎风转向，一起验证一下。
- Decide on your strategy for the beat—go one way, tack on the shifts, try to sail to the gusts or stay with the fleet? Or a combination of these?
- 制定迎风航段的策略——确定在哪一侧航行，遇阵风就迎风转向，试着往阵风区航行，还是保持和船群在一起？或者结合以上某几条策略？
- Return to the start and check the line bias and get a transit if there is one.
- 回到起航线，检查起航线偏差，可行的话，选择一个参照物。
- Make sure you check what the course board says and where the windward mark is.
- 务必仔细查看航线公告板，看清楚上风标的位置。

- Be ready to start your stopwatch and sync it on the preparatory signal.
- 准备启动秒表，和起航准备信号同步。

Now it is decision time—where to start? Match where you start to the strategy for your beat. For example:

现在是时候决定——从哪里起航？结合起航位置和迎风航段的策略。例如：

- If you want to go right, then start to the right of the fleet so it is easier to tack.
- 如果你想要在航线的右边航行，那就要开始航行到船群的右边了，这样更容易进行迎风转向。
- If it is a port-biased line and you need to go left, you might have to fight it out for the pin.
- 如果左端有利，那你就要航行到左边，你可能需要为左侧的位置进行一番争夺。
- If the wind has shifted left in the starting sequence, then you need to find a position on the line where you can tack early onto port.
- 如果在起航程序进行期间，风摆向了左边，那你就需要在起航线上找个好位置，确保能够尽早地迎风转向到左舷航行。

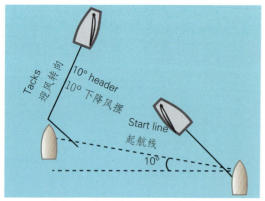

Most championship start lines have a 5–10° port-end bias: starting at port can give you an immediate advantage over the fleet; with a small header of around 10°, you can tack and cross them all!

在大多数锦标赛的起航线上，总会有5°～10°的偏差：左端起航有非常明显的优势；如果存在10°左右较小的下降风摆，你只要迎风转向，就能抢先出发，横穿整个船群！

Executing Your Start 起航执行

- Learn to be confident near the line. Sail up and down it; come up to it from below; drop down onto it from above.
- 培养在起航线上的操作自信。在两端来回航行；从起航线下方来到线上；从上方往下航行到起航线上。
- Identify the rate and angle of drift of the slowest possible starboard tack approach. Use this knowledge to get to your planned starting point at the starting signal.
- 以最慢的速度右舷航行接近起航线，明确漂移的速度和角度。运用这一信息，在起航信号发出时，航行到计划的起航点。
- Hold your position by filling your sail, gaining a little headway, then luffing until the boat stops. It will then start to slip back, so bear off, get headway again, and luff once more.
- 使主帆受风，稍微提速，保持位置，然后迎风偏转直到船停下来。这时候，船会往后漂，那就顺风偏转，再次提速往前，再迎风偏转一次。
- Try to squeeze the boats to windward. This will help keep your nose ahead, so your wind is clear and you keep luffing rights. Beware getting so close to the windward boat that it touches and gets stuck alongside you. All you can do in this situation is protest, and they have ruined your start. If you push them back in anger, you're DSQ! Try to stop the windward boats sailing over you. Keep your bow ahead, point high and hold them back.
- 试着把船往上风挤。这有助于你保持船头朝前，受风清晰，而且保有迎风偏转的权利。注意不要过于靠近上风侧的船，这可能会造成船只接触，使对方卡在你旁边。在这种情况下，你能做的只有抗议，因为他已经扰乱了你的起航。如果你因被干扰而把他们推开，就会被取消本轮资格！试着不要让上风船靠近你。保持船头向前，高角度向上，防止他们超过你。
- Use double tacking (see p49) to get into gaps to windward and keep clear water beneath you. Do a 'double' at every opportunity. Starboard tacks boats will intentionally be sailing very slowly and will not be in a

CHAPTER 6 第六章 Tactics 战术

position to speed up much to get you. Under RRS Rules 15 and 16 they may not alter course without giving you 'room to keep clear'. A loud hail of 'Hold your course' and / or 'Room please!' may well hold them back.

- 运用迎风双转（参见本书 54 页）在起航线上找到一个空位，来到上风侧，保持下风水域清晰。抓住一切机会去"迎风双转"。右舷船会故意慢速航行，但是他们无法加速阻碍你。根据《帆船竞赛规则》的第 15 和 16 条，他们不可以在没有给你"避让空间"的情况下改变航向。你只需要大声喊"保持你的航向"和 / 或"请给予空间"，就能很好地阻止他们超越你。

- Reaching along behind the fleet on port tack with a few minutes to go, hoping to find a way through to the front-line needs practice, a good nerve, and a lot of luck! It will not work in a big fleet of top competitors.

- 你也可以在起航倒计几分钟时，在船群下方左舷横风航行，试图找到一个空隙插到前排。掌握这种技巧需要经过大量练习，你必须足够大胆而且非常幸运。如果船只众多且高手如云，这种策略恐怕不会奏效。

- Make sure that you know the racing rules relating to the start perfectly; then make sure everybody around you knows that you are in control and they cannot push you around. Threaten the windward boats loudly; tell the starboard tackers to hold their course; demand 'room and time to keep clear' from leeward boats. Be noisy if necessary but keep cool!

- 确保自己熟知与起航相关的所有规则；然后让周围所有的水手都明白，一切都在你的掌控之下，他们无法左右你。大声威吓上风船；告诉右舷船保持他们的航向；要求下风船

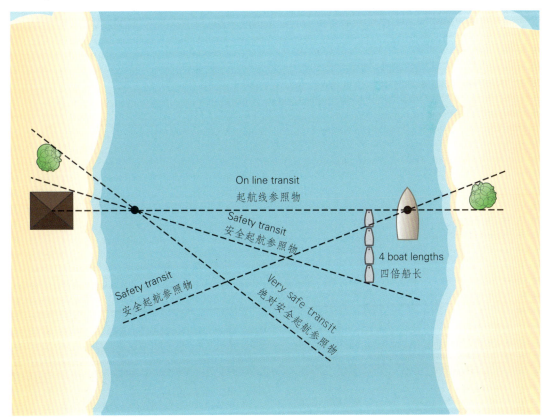

Getting transits
选取参照物

"给予空间和时间,避免碰撞"。如有必要,大声喊叫,但依旧保持冷静!

Surviving Black Or U Flag Starts!
黑旗或 U 旗起航

Think about how the fleet might react to a black or U flag. It is safer to start at an end because it is easier to tell where the line is. However, lots of sailors will think like this so the ends might get crowded. In the middle it is harder to tell where the line is, so sailors will be tentative. This often results in a large line sag and terrible starts out of the middle. If you can get a good transit and be confident, it is often easy to jump the fleet in the middle and have an easy, safe and good start.

思考一下船群会如何应对黑旗或 U 旗。从两端起航更安全一些,因为更容易辨别起航线的位置。不过,很多水手都会有相同的想法,从而使起航线两端变得非常拥挤。在中间的话,更难判断起航线的位置,所以中间的水手会显得犹豫不决。这通常会导致起航线呈下凹状态,以至于中间的船起航状态都很差。如果你能找到一个好的参照物,而且保持自信,通常能够很轻松地来到船群中间,确保自己有一个简单、安全、良好的起航。

Watch how the fleet lines up for the start and make your decision!

观察船群在起航线上的排列,做出自己的决定!

Do not keep sailing to windward if there is a general recall in a black flag start. Try not to get spotted as a premature starter by immediately stopping your boat; sit on the transom, ease the sheet and bear away.

在黑旗起航被集体召回时,不要一直往上风航行。尽量不要立即停船,以免被抓到抢航;坐到船尾,松缭,顺风偏转。

Optimist start lines are very congested
OP 比赛起航线上拥挤非凡

PRACTICE IDEAS 练习方法

Practising Starting 练习起航

Short line exercises can be used to develop close-quarter boat handling, rule knowledge and build confidence. Depending on the number of sailors, set a reasonably short line between two marks with a mark 50m to windward for turning. Practise with sound signals at 3 minutes, 2, 1, go.

短起航线练习能够帮助水手们发展近距离控船技巧、掌握规则运用，并提高自信。根据水手的人数，采用两个浮标设置一条足够短的起航线，并在上风50 m处设置一个转向标。起航的声音信号为 3 min、2 min、1 min、开始。

Alternative exercises are:
其他练习：

- Fight for the starboard end. The idea is to get into and hold the position on the line nearest to the starboard end.
- 抢占起航线右端。主要目的是，占领最靠近起航线右端的位置。
- Fight for the port end. The game is to attempt to get and hold the pin end position. This is virtually impossible, but is good practice for a slow controlled approach, tacking into gaps, and double tacking.
- 抢占起航线左端。目的是，占到左端的位置并保持。虽然基本上不太可能，但是很适用于练习慢速控船，迎风转向进入空位，和迎风双转。
- Place half the group on the line, and then with one minute to go the other half try to get into the front rank. To really congest the line, set up a box below the line outside which sailing is not allowed.
- 先让团队里一半的水手来到起航线上，过一分钟后，让另一半水手试着抢到前排。为了增加起航线的拥堵效果，可以在起航线下方设置一个方形区域，禁止水手们在区域外航行。

There are lots more variations of these exercises, so be creative and think about what you are trying to improve.

这些练习可以有很多变形，发挥你的创造力，考虑好你想提高哪些方面的技巧。

The Beat
迎风航段

First Half Of The Beat 迎风前半段

If you can go straight for the first few minutes after the start and you can make your own first decision without it being forced on you by the other boats, you have made a good start.

如果你能在起航前几分钟保持直线航行，并且在不受其他船压迫的情况下，做出自己的第一个决策，那就是一个非常好的起航了。

- Don't tack too often, and never (hardly ever!) in the first 100m.
- 不要频繁地迎风转向，尤其是在迎风段前 100 m内，绝对不要(几乎不需要)迎风转向。
- Follow your race plan. If your start has gone wrong, look for opportunities to get clear air and then quickly get back to your race plan.
- 遵循你的比赛计划。如果起航不好，就努力寻找机会，获得清晰的受风，并快速地找回自己的节奏，按比赛计划行事。
- Keep in clear air and sail fast.
- 保持受风清晰，快速航行。

Second Half Of The Beat 迎风后半段

- Keep away from the laylines and sail the 'middle cone' unless your plan was to go fully one side for a gain.
- 保持与方位线的距离，在中间锥形区（如下图）航行，除非你计划完全在另一边航行，以获得更大优势。
- Think about how much risk you are taking with the fleet. If you are with the leading group, stick with them and sail fast. If you

are in the pack, spot the opportunities for good shifts, gusts or clear air.
- 思考一下你和船群一起航行的风险有多大。如果你在领先队伍中，就和他们保持一致，快速航行。如果你在船群中间，就寻找机会，密切关注好的风摆、阵风或清晰的受风。
- As the mark approaches be careful to keep your air clear as the fleet compresses.
- 随着你逐渐靠近浮标，注意在船群互相挤压时，保持清晰的受风。

The first half of the beat will be crowded—keep in clear air
迎风段的前半段会非常拥挤——注意保持清晰的受风

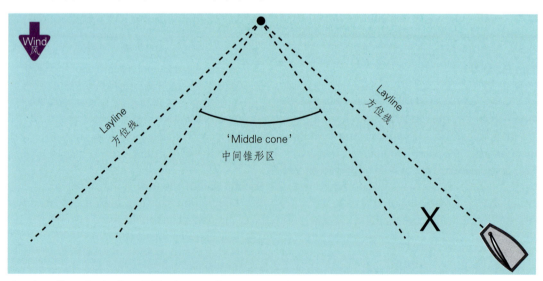

Don't sail on the layline: if lifted, you will overstand; if headed it may be difficult to tack and you might have to sail the header and lose distance
不要在方位线上航行：如果受上升风摆，你就会超出方位线；如果受下降风摆，你可能会很难迎风转向，不得不在下降舷航行，导致离标更远

CHAPTER 6 第六章 | Tactics 战　术

The Windward Mark
上风标

Windward Mark Approach 靠近上风标

- Get the boat dry before arriving at the mark.
- 在到达浮标前，将船内的水排完。
- With few boats near, you can sail fast with clear wind right up to the mark. Take your chance with a late approach. There is no need to get on the layline too early and risk a loss due to a windshift or misjudgement.
- 在周围没有太多船只的情况下，趁着受风清晰，快速航行来到浮标。抓住机会，但晚些接近方位线。没有必要过早，以免因风摆或错误的判断而失利。
- In the 'pack' there is lots to be gained and lost. If it is very crowded, then what can often work is to come up to the starboard layline earlier. Sail right through the layline, dipping below boats where necessary until you are sure that you can lay the mark easily. Tack and sail quickly to the mark over the boats back-winding and blanketing one another to leeward.
- 在船群中，你的排名波动会非常大。如果十分拥挤，可以考虑早些来到右舷的方位线上。按方位线航行，如有必要，保持在其他船下方航行，直到你非常确定能轻松地完成绕标。然后迎风转向，从上方穿过一群受尾风影响和在下风被盖住的船，快速驶向浮标。
- Never tack to leeward or in the middle of the starboard boats on the layline unless you are sure you can get around the mark. If you fail to lay the mark you may well have to gybe out.
- 绝对不要迎风转向到下风侧，或者在方位线上众多右舷船中迎风转向，除非你非常确定能成功绕标。如果无法绕标，你可能要顺风转向再绕一次。
- If you try to luff for the mark and fail, you will lose many places—remember an Optimist will never luff round a mark against the tide! If you are going to hit the mark, make sure you get around it then do a 360!
- 如果尝试迎风偏转绕标失败了，你会下降很

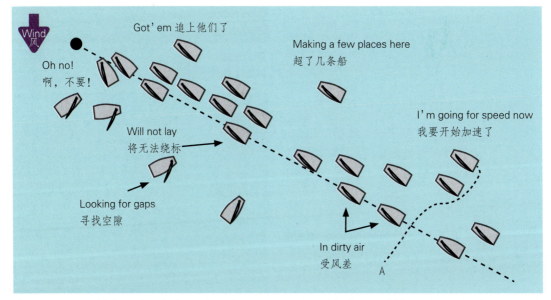

Stuck in the pack? Boat A sails through and past the starboard layline until it has clear wind. It then tacks and sails fast over the line of boats. They are all slowing one another, and some will get in trouble at the mark. Result—a few places gained.
因在船群中？A船航行超过右舷方位线，直到受风清晰。然后迎风转向，快速超过方位线上的船只。其他船都在相互拖慢彼此，有些船会在标旁遇到麻烦。A船最终会提高几个名次。

71

多名次——记住，OP 帆船绝对不可能逆流迎风偏转绕标！如果你要撞标了，确保在绕完标后再执行 360° 绕圈惩罚！

Rounding The Windward Mark 绕上风标

- Get onto the run quickly; every two lengths sailed on a broad reach is only one and a half lengths towards the leeward mark. Do, however, give port tack beating boats room to keep clear (RRS Rule 16).
- 快速转到顺风航行；侧顺风每航行两倍船长，往下风标的距离仅等同于 1.5 倍。无论如何，务必给左舷迎风航行的船只足够的避让空间（《帆船竞赛规则》第 16 条）。
- Stay on starboard tack until you have cleared the mark area, and then sail on the most direct route to the next mark (get a transit), keeping your wind clear!
- 保持右舷航行，直到驶离标区，然后以最直接的路线航行到下一标（运用参照物），注意保持受风清晰！
- It is often risky to gybe onto port straight away. There is less wind under all the boats on the starboard layline and a rules risk of a boat still coming upwind and having right of way. The only time this might work is when you are in last or the run is very biased to port gybe.
- 通常，立即顺风转向到左舷航行是非常冒险的。所有的船均在右舷方位线上，他们下方的风会很少，且均处于右舷航行，具有航行权。只有在一种情况下可行，你处于最后一名，或者在顺风航段上，左舷航行明显更有利。

The Reach
侧顺风航行

- If you are clear of groups, try to sail the straight-line course, using a transit if you can get one (ahead or behind).
- 如果你不受船群的影响，尽量直线航行。可行的话，找到一个参照物（前方或后方）。
- The first rule of reaching is 'don't get rolled'. The second rule of reaching is 'don't get rolled'! Go high if there is a bunch behind, but only high enough to keep your wind clear. Do this early and definitely: it will soon put the boats off trying to roll you.
- 侧顺风航行的第一准则是"不要被盖住"，第二准则是"不要被盖住"！如果后面跟了好几条船，往上风转，不过只需要转到受风足够清晰即可。尽早果断地转到高角度，这会很快打消其他船试图遮挡你的念头。
- Often it pays to go low if there is a bunch ahead. You might get room at the next mark

The reach
侧顺风航行

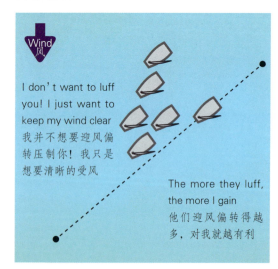

If there is no interference: sail straight for the mark
如无任何阻碍，直接驶向浮标

or even sail right under them if they get into a fight high.
- 通常，如果前面有好几条船的话，低角度航行会受益。你可能会在下一个标旁获得空间，甚至在其他船都在争抢高角度时，从他们正下方驶过。
- If you are heavy, ignore lightweight flyers coming up from astern. Psyche them into passing you well to windward with threats of luffing. Keep sailing the direct course. Keep low—let them go!
- 如果你体重较重，不要理会从船尾快速靠近的体重较轻的水手。威胁他们，你要迎风偏转遮挡他们，诱使他们从更靠上风的位置通过。你则继续保持直线低角度航行——让他们远离！
- Get on the inside at the mark. If you are 2nd or 3rd outside, get within three lengths of the mark and then slow down hard and dip around behind the inside boat.
- 占据浮标里侧的位置。如果你在外侧第二或第三的位置，驶进标旁三倍船长内的区域后努力减速，跟在里侧的船后面，从他们内侧贴标绕。

The Run
顺风航段

- Go for clear air, heading up or sailing by the lee to make sure you keep it
- 寻找清晰的风，迎风偏转或使帆与风同舷，保持受风清晰
- But seek to blanket the boats that are in front of you to slow them down
- 同时，也要尝试遮挡你前面的船，使他们减速
- Keep an eye out for stronger wind coming down behind you and make sure you get in it
- 密切留意后方吹来的强风，确保能进入强风区

Blanketing other boats will help you catch them up, but it can be quite difficult to overtake them. Getting into stronger wind first is more likely to help you overtake them.

遮挡其他船可以帮助你赶上他们，但却难以超过他们。抢先航行到更强的风区更有可能帮助你超船。

The run
顺风航段

The Leeward Mark
下风标

It is essential to start a beat from the inside position at the leeward mark. From any other position you have no immediate option of tacking clear and may have to sail for a long time in disturbed air. Like with the reach mark, if you are on the outside of a group, get within three boat lengths then slow down hard and dip round behind the inside boat. Watch out for boats ahead trying the same trick. If you were 'clear astern' of them at 'three lengths' you have no rights to room and will need to do an emergency stop.

在转到迎风航段之前，占据下风标里侧的位置非常重要。从任何其他位置，都无法立即迎风转向，获得清晰的受风，而且可能会在混乱的气流中航行很长一段时间。像绕侧顺转向标一样，如果你在船群外侧，就航行到三倍船长内的区域，然后使劲减速，从内侧的船后面贴标绕。当心你前面的船，他们可能会尝试同样的技巧。如果你处于三倍船长内"明显在后"的位置，将无权要求空间，需要紧急停船。

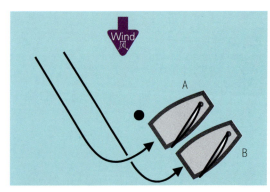

Round the mark so you leave it close (like A)
贴标绕（像 A 船一样）

The leeward mark
下风标

At the leeward mark: don't get caught on the outside
在下风标旁：注意不要被卡在外侧

The Gate
门标

You need to consider which mark to go around since one will almost certainly have an advantage. A good general rule is to consider the factors that might give an advantage in this order:

好好考虑绕哪一侧门标，因为一定会有一侧更有利。基本原则是思考哪些因素会带来优势，按以下顺序考虑：

- Gate bias (rounding one mark involves sailing less distance)
- 门标偏差（绕哪一侧门标所需航行的距离更短）
- Can you get the inside position or would you be stuck outside a group?
- 你能占领里侧的位置吗，还是会卡在船群外侧？
- Which way do you want to go up the beat—go round the mark sending you that way
- 你想从哪一侧航行迎风段——选择能带你去到那一侧的浮标
- Round the mark that puts you straight onto the lifted tack
- 选择能让你直接进入上升舷的那一侧门标

So, if there is noticeable bias, then take it; but if you can't tell there is any bias, then look for the mark that will give you an inside rounding. If you could round either mark clean, then go for the one that takes you to the favoured side of the beat or puts you straight onto the lifted tack.

因此，如果发现门标存在明显偏差，一定要好好利用；但是，如果你无法确定，就选择能够使你在内侧绕标的那一个。如果两边都可以顺畅地绕标，那就选择能让你转到迎风航段有利舷的一侧门标，或者能让你直接进入上升舷的那一侧门标。

The Finish
冲终点线

Finish To Windward 迎风冲线

It is easy to lose places at the finish. You must wrench your gaze from the opposition and force yourself to look at the line.

CHAPTER 6 第六章　Tactics 战　术

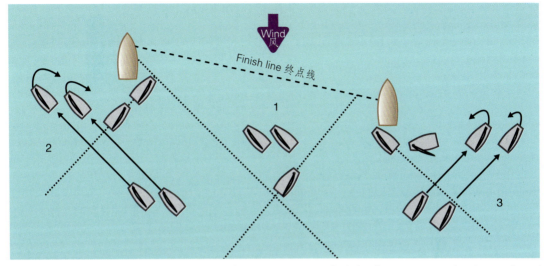

In Position 1, the boat sailing fast on port for the nearest end of the line may overtake the starboard tack pair who will sail further before finishing. In positions 2 and 3, the inner boat is blocking the outer boat from tacking for the line until the inner boat can tack and stay clear ahead.
在位置1处，左舷船正快速驶向终点线最近的一端，他可能会超过那两条右舷船，因为后者航行的距离更长些。在位置2和3处，里侧船挡住了外侧船，防止其迎风转向冲线，以便自己能够率先迎风转向，处于"明显在前"的位置。

冲终点线的时候很容易掉名次。你必须把目光从对手身上移开，努力让自己更多地关注终点线。

If you specialise in cool finishing you will nearly always make places. As you approach the line, ask yourself 'Which end is most downwind?' and then plan to approach that end at speed, preferably on starboard tack. On the approach, be careful you are not being blocked outside the layline and prevented from tacking.

如果你能在最后冲线时保持专注，几乎总能在最后多争取几个名次。当你接近终点线时，问问自己"哪一端更顺风一些？"然后全速冲过去，最好是右舷航行。在靠近过程中，注意不要因为卡在方位线外侧而无法迎风转向。

If the port end is nearest, tack onto the comfortable dead cert layline and sail for the pin, shouting loudly to put off anybody who may be thinking of trying to squeeze in between you and the mark.

如果左端更近，迎风转向到方位线上，确保方位线能使你顺利绕标。如有必要，在驶向左端的同时，大声叫喊，让任何想要插进你和左侧标之间的人打消念头。

If the starboard end is nearest, get over to the starboard layline fairly soon, unless there is a large finishing boat which is taking the wind close to it.

如果右端更近，就尽早来到右侧的方位线，除非终点船较大，遮挡了右侧的风。

Avoid being sailed up to the unfavoured port end of the line by boats to windward preventing you from tacking.

避免被上风船压制，导致你不能迎风转向，被挤到不利的终点线左侧。

When defending, try to sail an opponent out past the layline for the preferred end so you can control your approach to the finishing line.

在防守时，试着诱导对手去往有利的一侧，使其超出方位线，以便你控制靠近终点线的路线。

75

When sailing an opponent past the port end of the line, make sure you go far enough past the mark to prevent him getting an overlap when you both tack for the mark.

在使对手航行超过终点线左端时，确保超过的距离足够远，以防止他在你们同时迎风转向绕标时制造相联。

Reaching Finish 侧顺风冲线

The race isn't over until it's over. A lot can be lost on a final reach to the finish. Remember the first rule of reaching 'don't get rolled'.

不冲完终点线比赛就不算结束。在最后冲线的时候，可能会失掉很多名次。记住，侧风冲线的第一准则是"不要被盖住"。

When approaching a reaching finish, keep your wind clear and go for the nearest end. Try to see whether the line has been laid as you approach the leeward mark on the previous round.

在侧顺风靠近终点线时，保持受风清晰，驶向最近的一端。试着在冲线前一航段靠近下风标时，查看终点线是否已经设置好。

- If the windward end is nearest, go for the windward end, luffing if necessary
- 如果上风端更近，就驶向上风端，必要时可迎风偏转
- If the line is square go for the windward end, but if hassled by lightweight flyers, drop down and let them luff while you go for the leeward end with speed
- 如果起航线无偏差，则驶向上风端。但是如果受到很多体重较轻且航行快速的水手干扰，就转到他们下方航行，让他们迎风偏转，你则快速冲向下风端
- If the leeward end is nearest, then try to get to it but beware of slowing and being rolled
- 如果下风端更近，就试着往那一端航行，但注意你的速度要减慢，避免其他船只在你上风转向而盖住你

Running Finish 顺风冲线

To finish on a run, keep your wind clear, sail as straight as possible using a transit, and go for the nearest end. Try to sail your fastest angle as much as possible and not change your style to get to the finish — gybe if you have to.

顺风冲终点时，应保持受风清晰，运用参照物，尽可能直线航行，驶向最近的一端。尽量以最快的角度航行，保持这种航行方式，直到冲终点线——必要时顺风转向。

Sometimes you can use running by the lee on starboard to great advantage so you have right of way in a close finish.

有时可以顺风右舷航行，使帆与风同舷，以获得更大的优势。因为这样能保证你在冲线阶段，与其他船近距离对抗时拥有航行权。

EQUIPMENT & TUNING
装备 & 调试

PART 3 第三部分

CHAPTER 7 第七章
Mast Rake 桅杆倾度

Mast rake is the most mysterious element of rig control which has probably been blamed for more poor results than any of the other intangibles that go into making a successful race. What really matters is firstly that it is important in balancing the boat, and secondly that the skipper believes his rake is right.

桅杆倾度是索具控制中最神秘的因素。相比其他无形因素，桅杆的倾斜度设置不当，往往导致更糟糕的比赛结果。真正关键的是，首先桅杆倾斜对船的左右平衡起到重要作用；其次，船长必须相信自己的设置是正确的。

Measuring Mast Rake
测量桅杆倾度

Mast rake is measured from the mast head to the top of the boat's transom using the following method:

采用以下方法测量从桅顶到船尾板上端的距离，确定桅杆的倾斜度：

- Make sure the mast is at the back of the deck slot, and that the step is as far forward as it can move.
- 确保桅杆位于甲板槽后部，桅座已尽量往前。
- As most masts are now hollow-topped, hook the tape over the rim at the top of the mast.
- 由于现在的桅杆顶部大多数都是空心的，所以可以将卷尺钩在桅顶边缘。
- Extend the tape over the centre of the transom.
- 将卷尺拉长至船尾板中心。
- Take the reading, where the tape touches the transom. Readings are in the range 274–290 cm (108–114 in). The mast step should be calibrated with marks to show the mast rake so you can adjust the rake afloat.
- 读取卷尺与船尾板交界处的数据。读数范围为 274~290 cm（108~114 in）。应调节桅座上的刻度，确定相应的桅杆倾斜度，以便在水上进行调节。

Setting Mast Rake
设置桅杆倾度

The theory of balance and mast rake was discussed in Chapter 1: Speed Basics (see p12).

船的左右平衡和桅杆倾度理论在第一章有讨论过：基本速度理论（参见第 2 页）。

You can set the mast rake by feel:
你可以凭感觉来设置桅杆倾斜度：
- Too much weather helm, then put the mast further forward
- 如果感觉上风舵太多，就将桅杆往前倾一些
- The rudder feels too light then bring the mast back
- 如果感觉舵太轻，就将桅杆往后倾一些

The problem is that you can also change the feel by how you sit, how much heel you are sailing with, the angle of your daggerboard and how you have your sail set and sheeted.

问题在于，你的感觉会受各种因素影响。你在船上所坐的位置、航行时船的倾斜度、稳向板的角度以及帆和缭的设置等因素均会改变你的感觉。

It is identifying which of these factors needs to be changed to allow you to sail the boat perfectly in the groove that is important.

重要的是，明确以上哪些因素需要调节，

CHAPTER 7 第七章　Mast Rake 桅杆倾度

使你能够完美地航行。

A good starting point is to keep the COE of the sail consistent and then work with the other variables to develop the correct feel. The easiest way to do this is to set the boom so it is horizontal when you are sailing upwind. This can be done on the water and checked by the sailor and coach. This means that, as the wind increases, the mast is moved forward to counter the increased sheet tension and mast bend.

在初期可采用的一个好方法是，保持帆的受力中心不变，然后再调节其他变量，形成正确的感受。最简单的做法是，在迎风航行时，将横杆设置到水平。可在水上进行设置并和教练一起检查。这意味着，随着风力增强，应使桅杆往前倾，以抵消增强的主缭张力和桅杆弯曲度。

The calibration of the mast foot can be recorded so that an idea can be got as to what mast rake is required for different wind strengths. This means that a good guess can made by the sailor on the shore before they get on the water and check it.

记录桅座的调节数据，以便了解不同风力下所需的桅杆倾斜度。这样，水手在岸上调船时，就能很好地预估桅杆的设置，并在下水前进行检测。

When it goes very light, it often pays to bring the COE further back so that the rudder has some feel and gives you more feedback. This helps in the very light winds so that you can tell when the boat is driving well. In these conditions you can set up with the boom end pointing very slightly down.

当风很小时，通常将帆的受力中心进一步后移会更有益，舵感会更多，舵的反应也更快。这有助于在小风中判断航行是否顺利。在这些情况下，你可以将横杆末端略微往下调一些。

Some good starting numbers for the mast rake:

在航海起步阶段，可参考以下桅杆倾度数据：

Wind 风力	cm 厘米	in 英寸
Light 小风	274~279	108~110
Medium 中风	279~284	110~112
Heavy 大风	284~289	112~114

CHAPTER 8 第八章
Fast Gear 速航装备

The aim is to have the perfect combination of hull, sail, spars, toestraps and controls to suit the sailor. The competitor must make his boat as individual and comfortable as his favourite trainers—but first, get a copy of the class rules and read them carefully. You will then know what you can and cannot do.

目标是使船体、船帆、杆件、压舷带和控制装置完美地结合起来,以满足水手的需求。选手必须使自己的船使用起来更加舒适,也更适合自己,如同自己最喜欢的运动鞋——但是首先,应获取所用船型的级别规则并仔细阅读。这样你就知道什么能做,什么不能做。

You need to be comfortable in your boat to get the maximum out of it
太舒服地在船上驾驶,最大限度地发挥其性能

Hull
船体

Buy a new or well cared for Optimist one-design which is at the minimum weight.

OP 为统一设计船型。在选购时,应购买一个全新的或保养良好的船体,并且符合最低重量要求。

Keep it smooth and clean with sharp edges to the transom and the aft third of the chine. Smooth with 600 grade wet and dry paper, finishing with 1200 grade or polishing paste. Regularly clean and degrease with washing up liquid. Scratches and bangs can be repaired with gelcoat filler.

保持船体的平滑和清洁,将船尾板和舭缘线后 1/3 处边缘打磨锋利。首先用 600 目干湿砂纸进行打磨,最后用 1 200 目砂纸或抛光膏处理。定期用洗涤液清洗并除油。用胶衣填充剂修复船体划痕和损伤。

Always use a well-padded trolley and never let the hull touch anything else. When turning your boat over, use two people: one at each end. Turn the boat in one swinging movement through at least 90°, putting it down on the gunwale if you cannot turn through 180° in one movement.

OP 的船车必须装有加厚的衬垫,使用时不要让船体触碰任何其他物体。如需翻转船体,要两人合作,一人一端。每次至少转动 90°,如无法一次转动 180°,则船舷着地放下。

After use, rinse the hull with freshwater, clean and dry it, and cover the bottom with a soft and preferably padded cover.

使用后，应用淡水冲洗船体，清洁并晾干，最后用柔软的船罩盖住底部。船罩最好是带衬垫的。

Make sure your hull is smooth with sharp edges
确保船体光滑且边缘棱角清晰

Daggerboard
稳向板

Suitable foils are of vital importance to get optimum performance. Like the hull, foils must be close to the minimum weight and should be kept perfectly smooth and clean.

合适的板件（稳向板和船舵）装备是最佳航行的关键。像船体一样，板件必须接近最低重量要求，且保持表面完全光滑和清洁。

The daggerboard controls leeway and acts as the pivot through which your hiking balances the force from the sails. If the board is 'soft'(flexible) it will bend, and you will lose 'feel' and drive. However, there is an advantage in having a board that bends just a little in heavy weather in the biggest gusts and waves, to act as a shock absorber helping the sailor keep the boat flat and under control. Light helms need a daggerboard that is more flexible, bending under the lighter loadings they can exert. Heavier helms need progressively stiffer daggerboards, and sailors over 55kg need a totally rigid board.

稳向板控制航行的偏航程度。在水手需要平衡风力进行压舷时，它还是压舷的轴点。如果稳向板很"软"（易弯曲），就会被压弯，你就无法"感知"船的动向，并失去航行的动力。但是，在遇到大风大浪这样剧烈的天气状况时，如果稳向板稍微弯曲一点，对航行更有利。它能减少航行的震动，更有利于水手压舷和控船。体重轻的舵手需要一块更易弯曲的稳向板，能在较轻的负载下弯曲，使他们能够更好地航行。舵手的体重越重，所需稳向板应越硬。体重超过55公斤的水手则需要一块完全坚硬的稳向板。

The daggerboard and its box should match. The daggerboard construction and tolerances are now very small since the rules were tightened in 2005. To match the board, the daggerboard case should be packed to as narrow as possible, the minimum being 14mm. The packing must be uniform and within 30mm of the top and bottom of the case. This ensures:

稳向板和稳向板槽必须完全匹配。自2005年规则收紧以来，稳向板的制造和允许偏差就非常严格了。为了和板相吻合，稳向板槽应填充得越窄越好，填充厚度最小为14 mm。槽内的填充物厚度应一致，距槽上下30 mm。

这确保：

- The daggerboard will not wobble from side to side in the box, making steering jerky and affecting your 'feel'
- 稳向板不会在槽内左右晃动，影响掌舵的稳定性和你的"船感"
- As little water as possible is trapped in the box-water in the box adds to the boat's mass
- 最大限度地减少船内积水——槽内的水会增加船的重量
- Minimal turbulence occurs where the daggerboard and hull meet

81

- 最大限度地降低稳向板和船体的交接处出现湍流的情况

The rules allow stops to be fitted in the ends of the top and bottom openings of the case. These prevent the edges of the foil from being damaged, and also allow you to alter the rake of the board.

规则允许在稳向板槽开口处的前后端安装防撞条。不仅可以防止稳向板边缘受损，也方便水手调整稳向板的倾斜度。

The aft bottom stop should be of maximum length (30mm) with a V cut into it to take the foil's edge. Other stops should be no bigger than 5 mm. High density rubber glued in place with Sikaflex is very satisfactory.

后底部防撞条应采用最大长度（30 mm），切割成"V"形槽，以包裹稳向板边缘。其他防撞条不应长于 5 mm。使用高密度橡胶条，用西卡胶进行固定，效果会非常好。

The daggerboard's rake can be controlled with a loop of elastic cord fixed to the sides of the case by two eyelets. This allows the board to be raked forward, back, or held vertical in the box to improve balance.

稳向板的倾斜度可通过一圈弹性绳来控制，弹性绳则通过两个孔固定在稳向板槽两侧。这样可使稳向板前后倾斜，或在槽中保持竖直，提高其稳定性。

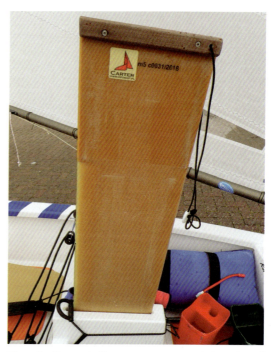

The elastic cord allows you to control the rake of the board
弹性绳控制稳向板倾斜度

Stops fore and aft of the daggerboard case
稳向板槽前后两端的防撞条

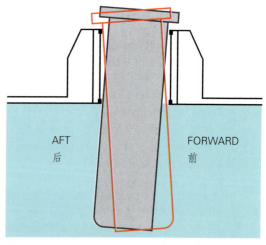

The daggerboard can be raked slightly forward or aft
稳向板可小幅度前后倾斜

CHAPTER 8 第八章 **Fast Gear 速航装备**

> **TOP TIPS 几点建议**
>
> Beware! Hot sun can warp foils. Keep them out of the sun or, if possible, in padded bags.
>
> 注意！强烈的光照会使稳向板和舵叶变形。注意避免在阳光下暴晒，尽量将其存放在加厚的储存袋中。

Use a padded bag to protect your foils
使用带厚衬垫的储存袋存放，以保护稳向板和舵叶

Rudder
船舵

The rudder has a lot of work to do:
舵的作用很多：

- It transmits the feel of the water and signals the state of balance of the boat to the helmsman
- 舵会传递水的流动，并向舵手传达船的平衡状态
- It is the means of controlling the boat
- 舵是船的控制装置

To perform these functions, it is essential that both rudder blade and head are as stiff as possible so there is little or no twist between tiller and blade.

为了发挥这些功能，关键是舵叶和顶部都越坚硬越好，从而尽可能地减少舵柄和舵叶之间的扭曲。

In the original class rules, the rudder blade rules were very loose. The rudder only had to fit in a rectangle. This meant that all sort of rudder rakes and designs were tried.

在最初的级别规则中，舵叶的相关规则是非常宽松的。只需保证船舵不超过规定的矩形盒体即可，这就意味着人们可以对舵的倾斜度和设计进行各种尝试。

In 1995 these rules started to be tightened up. Since 2005 the rule has become very precise, allowing very little tolerance or change of materials. This makes it a lot easier to buy a good rudder. Be careful if you have an old boat since your rudder might not measure for racing under the current rules. An old-style rudder will also feel very different and alter your boat handling. So, even if you are a relatively new racer, it is worth getting a current-style rudder as soon as you can.

1995年，这些规则开始收紧。自2005年以来，规则变得非常精确，允许的偏差或材料的选择空间变得很小。这一举措使人们更容易买到好的船舵。注意，如果你的帆船年代比较久远的话，你的船舵可能并不满足现行的比赛规则。而且老式的船舵使用起来感觉很不一样，还会改变你的控船方式。所以，即使作为一个比赛新手，你也应尽早配置一个新式的船舵。

Tiller & Tiller Extension 舵柄 & 副舵柄

For the tiller, a length of 600–650 mm seems about right: too long and it gets in the way, too short and the steering gets heavy.

就舵柄而言，600~650 mm的长度基本就够了：过长的话，会阻碍在船上的操作；过短的话，则会使舵变得很沉。

The tiller extension should be as long as possible to a combined maximum of 1 200 mm. Do keep an eye on the universal joint for wear and tear. It can fail quickly—which is a disaster!

83

副舵柄则应越长越好，加上舵柄最长为 1 200 mm。时常检查万向节，该部件一旦出现损伤，就会马上坏掉——这是个大麻烦！

Mast
桅杆

For speed and high pointing, all sailors need as stiff a mast as possible. The mast thwart sleeve must hold the mast snugly athwartships, allowing maximum legal fore-and-aft movements (3mm). The mast step must have a very snugly fitting track to prevent any side-to-side movement, but the step adjuster must allow the step to slide back and forward over the maximum permitted range (3mm).

为了提高船速和航行角度，水手们应尽可能选择坚硬的桅杆。桅杆底座袖筒必须能将桅杆左右固定，按照规定前后最多允许移动 3 mm。桅座的槽必须刚好贴合桅杆，防止其左右移动。但是桅座调节器必须能使桅座前后滑动，允许的最大范围为 3 mm。

- The sprit tackle must be strong, with low friction blocks, a good handle and the cleat positioned where it can be adjusted easily. There are two commonly used cleat positions:
- 斜撑杆滑轮装置应十分牢固，滑轮摩擦力要小。要有一个好用的把手，卡绳器的位置也要易于调节。以下两个位置十分常用：
- The first position, and probably the most common, is below the lower sail tie and has to be adjusted by a bouncing technique from a standing position, pushing downwards on the handle with all your body weight. Using a long low-stretch rope from the mast block to the lower block at gooseneck level minimises windage and turbulence over the sail luff. Light and inexperienced helms may struggle with this system but it can be good for the stronger heavier sailors.
- 第一个位置很可能是最常见的，位于下端绑帆绳下方。水手要站起来，使用全身重量，使劲往下推把手进行调节。应采用一段较长的低弹性绳，先绕桅杆上滑轮，再到万向节处的下滑轮，最大限度地减少风阻和帆前缘处的乱流。体重较轻且缺乏经验的舵手可能会难以适应这种系统；但对于体重较重且强壮的水手来说，则非常友好。
- The other cleat position is some 40cm below the mast block. This allows the helm to lean forward, sitting on the buoyancy bag / tank / side deck, and pull down on the handle. All sailors find this system easy to use. There is some windage penalty but, in most cases, this is more than made up for by better sail setting.
- 另一个位置是，桅杆上滑轮下方约 40 cm 处。这样便于舵手坐在浮力袋（气袋）/ 舱 / 船舷甲板上，身体往前倾，往下拉把手。水手们都觉得这种装置非常好用。虽然可能会产生一些风阻，但是在大多数情况下，可以更好地调节帆的设置，从而弥补损失。

The common sprit tackle arrangement and cleat position just below the lower sail tie

常见的斜撑杆滑轮设置，卡绳器位于下端绑帆绳下方

The sprit tackle is a common site of gear failure, which inevitably results in retirement. Carry a spare top block and a length of low stretch rope for rapid repairs.

斜撑杆的滑轮设置很容易出问题，一旦发生就会直接导致退赛。水手可以携带一个备用上滑轮和一段低弹性绳，用于快速修理。

The sprit tackle being adjusted on the water
在水上调节斜撑杆滑轮设置

> **TOP TIP** 重要提示
>
> Change the sprit rope regularly else it will harden and wear at the cleating point.
>
> 定期更换斜撑杆固定绳，卡绳点很容易变硬且磨损。

The typical sprit tackle arrangement
典型的斜撑杆滑轮设置

Top Ties
上端绑帆绳

These must be very strong as they take the enormous thrust of the sprit transmitted down the headrope. If they stretch, your leech tension varies, and the throat may move further from the mast than allowed by the rules (more than 10 mm).

这里必须绑得非常牢固，因为此处会承受斜撑杆往下挤推上帆边绳的巨大推力。如果绑得不紧，受力后拉伸，帆后缘的张力就会改变，而且帆喉可能会离桅杆更远，超出规则允许的范围（超过 10 mm）。

The Optimax and Optipart systems involve plugs which go in the top of the mast which the horizontal and diagonal ties attach to. The plugs also have holes which sit inside the mast to hold the wind indicator or burgee in place.

Optimax（OP 杆件品牌）和 Optipart（OP 部件品牌）系统采用插销的形式，两个插销分别位于桅杆上端绑帆绳和斜绑绳固定处。插销在桅杆里侧的部位有孔，可用于固定风向指示器或三角旗。

These systems are efficient but some find them difficult to adjust. Use Dyneema or Spectra of 3 mm diameter and check ties for each major event and heavy weather races and replace if necessary. Watch for wear where the cringle rubs and where the ties go into the mast.

这些系统很高效，但同时有些人发现很难对其进行调节。绑绳应使用直径 3 mm 的大力马绳或斯百克线，在每次大型活动或者剧烈天气情况下比赛都必须进行检查，必要时及时更换。注意检查帆眼摩擦处以及绑帆绳在桅杆里侧的磨损情况。

Alternatively, you can use a simpler system, passing the ties through the holes in the mast, around the wind indicator / burgee and back out again, securing and adjusting them with simple, dependable and easily adjustable knots!

或者你可以使用一种更简单的系统，将绑

绳穿过桅杆上的孔，缠绕风向标/三角旗，然后再穿回来，最后采用简单牢固、易调节的绳结进行固定并调整。

Whatever system is used, the key is for it to be adjustable and non-stretch.

无论使用什么系统，关键是可调节且不会延伸。

Boom
横杆

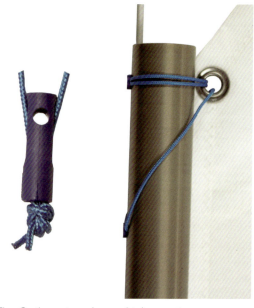

The Optimax top pins and tying system
Optimax 上端插销和绑绳系统

Boom stiffness is essential to keep the sail flat in heavy weather and control the leech. A bendy boom will slacken the leech in gusts but will result in the sail becoming slightly fuller. Mast, sprit bend and sail cut allow the leech to fall off adequately in gusts for most sailors, complementing the use of sprit and kicking strap (vang).

横杆的硬度可以在剧烈天气下保持帆的平整，对控制帆后缘很关键。弯曲的横杆会使帆后缘在阵风中变得松弛，但会使帆稍微饱满一些。对于大多数水手来说，桅杆、斜撑杆的弯曲和帆形能使帆后缘在遇到阵风时，卸掉适当的风力，配合斜撑杆和斜拉器的使用。

Lighter sailors should consider using a boom which bends more to make the rig have greater automatic gust response and hence make the boat easier to sail.

体重较轻的水手应考虑使用更易弯曲的横杆，在结构上使帆和索具能够更好地应对阵风，从而使船更易航行。

All modern booms have special end fittings allowing minimum-friction double-purchase outhauls to be rigged. The rope must be low stretch. The outhaul cleat should be fitted in the middle of the boom where it can be reached easily on most points of sailing.

所有的现代横杆都配备特殊的末端部件，以便安装横拉器滑轮装置，最大限度地减小摩擦。横拉器必须使用低弹性绳。卡绳器必须固定在横杆中间，以便于航行时从各角度进行调节。

A boom uphaul loop (tack diagonal tie) must be fitted to the jaws. It slips over the pin on the front of the mast above the boom, controlling luff tension and length. To raise the boom and

A simpler system using rope through the holes and around the mast
一种更简单的系统，用绳子穿过帆眼，绕过桅杆

slacken the luff, simply twist the loop a few times before hooking it on.

横杆上拉环（前帆角斜绑绳）应穿过横杆插头，卡在桅杆前面横杆上部的销钉上，控制帆前缘的张力和长度。如要抬起横杆，松掉帆前缘，只需将上拉环扭转几次，卡在销钉上即可。

A strop spanning the middle half of the boom will reduce the boom bend but must not extend more than 10cm from the boom as this is the maximum the rules allow. The point where the mainsheet attaches to the strop is important. In light airs this needs to be just above the back of the daggerboard case. This allows you to keep your weight forward during tacks. In windier conditions the attachment point should be vertically above ratchet block. You can either have 2 separate rings or a single ring that can be slid along the strop. You can't move this attachment point while you are racing.

横杆三角绳位于横杆中部，长度约为横杆的一半，能减少横杆的弯曲程度，但是延伸长度不得超过10 cm（规则允许的最大值）。主缭与三角绳的连接点十分重要。在小风天，连接点应调节至稳向板槽后端正上方，以便在迎风转向时，保持重心靠前。在大风天，连接点则应位于主滑轮上方，与其垂直。连接处可采用两个分开的环或一个可在三角绳上滑动的单环。比赛时你不能移动连接点。

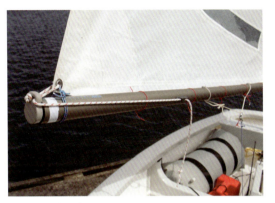

Boom outhaul system
横杆横拉器系统

Boom outhaul being adjusted while sailing
水手在航行时调节横拉器

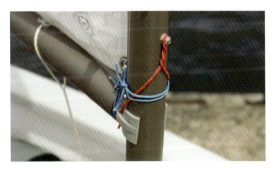

Tack diagonal tie
前帆角斜绑绳

Boom strop for mainsheet attachment—here the attachment is forward, but it would move back in windier conditions
用于连接主缭的横杆三角绳——图中的连接点位置靠前，在大风条件下则会靠后些

Mainsheet
主帆缭绳

This should be attached to the boom strop with a quick-release clip. Only ball bearing blocks should be used. The upper becket block should attach to the clip with a length of dynema, to minimise the amount of mainsheet needed. The ratchet block must be dependable and the switch to engage the ratchet must not jam or slip. A lightweight sheet is best in light weather but beware of a freshening wind! Use or carry a pair of gloves. The purchase on the mainsheet is really down to sailor size.

采用快挂装置将主帆缭绳固定在横杆三角绳上。只能使用滚珠滑轮，再用一段大力马绳将上滑轮系在快挂上，以尽量减少所需的主缆。检查并确保棘齿滑轮耐用可靠，棘齿的开关不能卡住或打滑。小风天使用轻型缭绳是最好的，但是要注意风势陡增！建议使用手套控缭或至少携带一副备用。主缆的绕绳圈数完全取决于水手的体格。

For smaller sailors it is worth making the system 4:1
对于体格较小的水手，有必要将系统调整为4:1

Consider tapering the sheet but make sure the thicker part never gets to the ratchet block. You can even taper the far end of the sheet and tie it to the back of the toestrap to save weight and reduce the risk of knots in the mainsheet.

考虑使用逐渐变细的主缆，但要确保粗的部分不会通过棘齿滑轮。你甚至可以将主缆末端编细，然后将其系到压舷带的后端，以减轻绳子的重量，降低主缆打结的风险。

3:1 mainsheet, suitable for larger sailorst
主缆设置比例为3:1，适合体格较大的水手

The 4:1 system can be rigged by tying or clipping the mainsheet to the becket to allow you to drop this down to a 3:1 in lighter winds.

4:1系统设置：使用绳子或用快挂将主缆固定在上滑轮上，以便在小风天将设置降为3:1。

A tapered mainsheet, with a thicker diameter for the part you hold
逐渐变细的主缆，手握部分会更粗些

Kicking Strap (Vang)
斜拉器

The kicking strap (vang) is usually made up of two ropes. An initial Dyneema rope from the boom to a loop through which a larger diameter, softer rope is attached and led through the cleat and wrapped over the boom to make it easier to use.

斜拉器通常由两段绳子组成。一根大力马绳绕过横杆，在末端绳圈处与一根更粗的软绳相连，软绳通过绳圈，穿过卡绳器，然后绕过横杆，让使用更容易。

Change the softer rope regularly otherwise it will harden and wear at the cleating point.

定期更换软绳，否则绳子会越来越硬，在卡绳点出现磨损。

The kicking strap
斜拉器

Toestraps
压舷带

Get the right position and tension. Tight straps maximise the rate of response of the boat to helm movement and reduce knee bend.

固定在合适的位置，调节好松紧程度。拉紧的压舷带能最大限度地提高船对舵手压舷的反应，并减少膝盖的弯曲程度。

If you are bigger with longer legs, consider having toestraps which meet close behind the ratchet block to make them further from the gunwale. If you are small, make sure the toestraps are pulled out to the side of the boat so you can get your bottom over the side easily.

如果你的体格大且腿长，可以考虑将压舷带固定到靠近主滑轮的位置，距船舷更远；如果你的体格较小，则确保压舷带能拉伸到船边，以便你轻松地将臀部移到船外。

Have the toestraps held up by elastic so it's easy to slip your feet under them after a tack or gybe.

使用弹性绳固定压舷带，以便你在迎风转向或顺风转向后，能够轻松地将脚收回到压舷带下方。

Toestraps for the smaller sailor, held up by elastic
小体格水手的压舷带设置，使用弹性绳固定

Hiking Pants
压舷裤

Padded trousers or strap-on pads make hiking much more comfortable. They should not be worn in light weather as they make it harder for you to move easily and feel what the boat is doing. Also make sure there isn't too much of a bump at the edges of the pads as this can make sliding in and out difficult.

在压舷时，穿上带衬垫的裤子或绑上垫子会

更舒适。但是不要在小风时候穿着这样的装备，会导致你在船上行动不便，而且无法感受船的动向。另外，确保衬垫的边缘平滑，无过多的凹凸部分，否则会使你在船舷上的滑动变得很困难。

Painter
缆绳

IOCA rules require at least 8 m of 5 mm buoyant rope. Attach to the mast foot, tie a loop 40 cm up the line (on which to tie painters of boats being towed astern) and stow under a buoyancy strap amidships. Praddles, sandwiches, water bottles, and so on should all be stowed amidships and not in the ends of the boat.

IOCA（国际OP级别协会）规定要求，缆绳至少是8 m长、5 mm粗的浮力绳。将它固定在桅底，在绳子上系一个40 mm的环（以便从船尾拖船时使用），然后将其存放在船中部的浮力袋绑带下方。桨、食物、水瓶等均需存放在船中部，而不是船尾处。

Compass
指南针

A compass is not essential, but it can be a very useful tool when sailing at sea with few landmarks to help spot the shifts. The most popular is the spherical Silva compass.

指南针不是必需的，但在海上航行没有陆标的情况下，指南针对于发现风摆会非常有用。最受欢迎的是席尔瓦球形指南针。

The Silva is usually mounted on the vertical face of the mast thwart in the mid-line. It has a simple mounting bracket which enables it to be removed when not in use. It operates accurately at all angles of heel and has a magnified black card with a Degree Scale in white and a Tactical Scale in yellow.

席尔瓦指南针通常安装在中间线桅杆底座的垂直面上。配有一个简单的固定支架，以便在不使用时拆除。在各种倾斜角度下均能准确运行。其黑色表盘具有放大功能，表盘上的度数刻度是白色的，战术刻度则是黄色的。

The Tactical Scale is read behind the sight line nearest the windward side of the boat. The scale is designed so that, when the boat tacks through 90°, the difference between the readings on the two tacks is 10—e.g. Port: 8; Starboard: 18.

在最靠近船上风侧的标记线处读取战术刻度上的数据。刻度的设计理念是：船迎风转向90°时，左右舷的读数差值为10——例如：左舷：8；右舷：18。

On starboard tack, when the wind lifts and the boat points higher, the reading on the Tactical Scale decreases. When headed the reading increases. On port tack the opposite is true: when lifted the reading increases, when headed it decreases. Mark the sides of the bulkhead with a reminder! Note that each unit on the Tactical Scale is 18 degrees, so even a half unit shift is quite significant.

在右舷航行时，遇到上升风摆，船能更迎风，战术刻度上的读数减小；遇到下降风摆时，读数则会变大。左舷航行则正好相反：遇上升风摆时，读数变大；遇下降风摆，读数变小。可在舱壁的两侧做记号提醒自己。注意，战术刻度上的每一大格代表18°，因此，即使是半格的风摆也是相当显著的。

The popular spherical Silva compass
大受欢迎的席尔瓦球形指南针

WIND & CURRENT
风 & 流

PART 4 第四部分

CHAPTER 9 第九章
Seeing The Wind 看 风

With a bit of imagination, the wind can be visualised flowing over and around everything. It slips over water, jumping from wave top to wave top, with little eddies in the troughs. It is slowed and deflected by friction as it rubs over land and sea, mountains and forests, farmland and lakes. The wind finds the easiest route to flow around obstacles, just like water moving over rocks in a stream.

发挥一点想象力，想象风在一切事物周围流动的样子。它可以在水面上滑行，从一个浪尖跳到另一个浪尖，在浪谷中形成小漩涡。当风吹拂过陆地和海洋、山川和森林、农田和湖泊，从而变慢而且转向。风会找到绕过障碍物的最简单的路径，就像溪水穿过岩石一样。

Imagine yourself sailing a course with headlands, moored ships, valley inlets and a patch of forest near the water. Use the wind bends to get to the windward mark first, and always sail towards the centre of a bend.

想象你正在水上航行，航线上有海岬、停泊的船只、山谷的入口和一片临水的森林。利用风的弯曲首先航行到迎风标，并始终朝弯曲中心航行。

Feel the wind on your face. Is it blowing harder on one cheek than the other? Can you feel it on your ears? When it cools both sides equally, you are facing dead upwind. Hear the wind. Look upwind and move your head slowly from side to side. When you can hear it whistling equally in both ears, you are looking dead upwind.

感受风拂过你的脸庞。风在一侧脸颊是否比另一侧脸颊更猛烈？你能感觉到它吹在耳朵上吗？当你感觉到两边耳朵都变冷时，那就说明你面朝着正迎风方向。听风声，看向迎风方向，缓慢地左右移动头部。当两耳都能听到同样的呼啸声时，那就说明你正看向正迎风方向。

See the wind on the water. You will see ripples being blown downwind. On smooth water these ripples are exactly at right angles to the surface wind. On rougher water you will see most ripples on the tops of waves where

When sailing in an estuary or river you have to imagine how the wind blows over hills, through trees, or past ships lying at an angle to the wind; always sail towards the centre of a wind bend

在河口或河流中航行时，需要想象风是如何吹过山丘、穿过树木，或掠过与风成一定角度的船只的；始终朝着风的弯曲中心航行

the wind strikes. As the surface wind varies, the ripples in each group will be from a slightly different direction, but they can still give a good overall indication of the wind direction.

观察水面上的风,你会看见顺风吹起的涟漪。在平静的水面上,水波与水面上的风完全成直角。在波涛汹涌的水面上,你会看到大部分波纹出现在风吹过的浪尖。随着水面风的变化,每组波纹的方向会略有不同,但依旧能很好地指示大体的风向。

On freshwater in strong winds, foamy lines can be seen going dead downwind on the water's surface. Seen from a height these can map out the airflow over a lake, showing wind bends.

强风天在淡水区域航行,能在水面上看到往正顺方向漂浮的泡沫线。从高处看,就像泡沫绘制出了湖面上空的气流图,显示风的曲线流动。

Gusts 阵风

Gusts can be seen as dark patches on the water, with bigger waves sometimes breaking with white flashes of foam. Look at the patterns gusts make when they hit the water. First you see a dark circular patch where the gust strikes. Then dark lines run out from it in all directions as the supercharged wind explodes outwards. You may also see areas where there is consistently more wind, maybe where it is funnelling down a valley or accelerating around a headland.

阵风在水面上呈黑压压的一片,伴有更大的波浪,有时还会出现白色的泡沫。观察阵风撞击水面时形成的图案。首先,你会看到阵风袭来的地方有一块黑色的圆斑。然后,随着风力增长向外爆发,黑线从圆斑向四面八方延伸。你可能还会看到有的区域风一直很多,其原因可能是风掠过山谷时加速,或绕过岬角速度上升。

In gusty weather keep an eye open to windward. When you see the tell-tale dark patch of a gust approaching, try to see which way it is moving:

在阵风天气,应注意观察上风侧。当你看到一片黑色的阵风逼近时,试着看清它的移动方向:

- If it is moving head on towards you, the wind escaping from it will head you: tack and you will get an enormous lift.
- 如果阵风正朝着你吹过来,周围溢出的风会使你下降:这时候迎风转向会获得很大的上升优势。
- If the gust is to the side of you and moving towards you over your shoulder, as it hits you are likely to get a lift: be ready to head up and sit out hard!
- 如果阵风朝着你的肩膀,从侧面吹过来,在抵达你时,你会获得很大的上升风力:准备好迎风偏转,坐到船外,努力压舷!

How to react to a gust
如何应对阵风

Anticipating The Wind 风况预测

Besides looking at the course and imagining how the wind will blow over it, look at the clouds. The lower clouds are of vital importance in predicting the wind.

除此之外,观察航线,想象风会如何从整个航线上吹过。还要观察云的状态,低层云对于风况预测至关重要。

Dark rain clouds usually mean air is dropping
乌云密布通常意味着空气正在下降

Cumulus clouds mean air is rising
积云意味着空气正在上升

Under a puffy white cumulus cloud the air is going up, so there will be less wind and it tends to back (shift to the left). As the cloud passes, faster air gusts down from the higher 'gradient' wind to replace the hot air rising in the cloud. This wind will be stronger and veered (shifted to the right). This shift effect would be reversed in the southern hemisphere.

在蓬松的白色积云下,空气上升导致风减少,并倾向于逆时针偏转(摆向左边)。随着云经过,空气快速从高处的"梯度"风中下沉,取代云层中上升的热空气。这时产生的风会更强,并且顺时针偏转(摆向右边)。这种偏转效应在南半球是相反的。

So, as a cloud approaches, sail on port as the wind drops and goes left; after it passes, sail on starboard through the fresher veered wind. Look for gusts coming down through the blue gaps between these clouds (stronger and veered).

所以当云接近时,风势减弱向左偏转,应左舷行驶;在云经过后,风更大、更清新且顺时针偏转,应右舷航行。留意云层中的蓝色间隙处吹来的阵风(更强且顺时针偏转)。

Dark clouds, which may have rain falling from them, are normally dropping cold air out of them. This will show as a gust or squall on the water. The gusts fan out from the cloud so, if the cloud is to the right of you, the wind will pull right and lift you on starboard. If the cloud is to the left of you, the lift will be on port.

乌云通常会释放冷空气,可能会形成降雨。在水面上则表现为阵风或暴风雨。阵风从云中扩散开来,如果云在你的右侧,风就会摆到右侧,右舷为上升舷;如果云在左侧,则左舷为上升舷。

Be careful; not all clouds are growing and sucking air up or reducing and dropping air down. A lot of clouds are fairly dormant, or are too high, and have little effect on the wind at ground level. So, try to use the cloud as an indicator but also look for the tell-tail signs of gusts on the water.

注意:并非所有的云都会增长并把空气向上吸,或减少使空气下沉。许多云处于休眠状态或者位置过高,对地面的风影响很小。因此,试着将云作为风向指示器的同时,也要寻找水面上阵风的痕迹。

Sails Bending The Wind 帆对风的影响

Imagine the airflow around an Optimist sail when going upwind. A boat on the same tack to leeward or a little behind will be headed by the turned wind and will slow down. A boat close to the windward quarter will also be slowed down, both by striking the wash and by being headed by the deflected wind. A boat on the other tack crossing the stern of our boat will get a lift from the turned wind.

想象一下迎风航行时 OP 船帆周围的气流。同舷航行的下风船或稍稍落后的船会被角度变化的风所影响，从而减速。靠近下风船上风角落的船也会受影响而减速。这些船都会撞击浪花，受风的影响而下降。在另一舷航行的船则能顺利从我们的船尾通过，利用风的偏转获得上升优势。

The wind being bent by a sail on the beat
在迎风航段，风遇到帆后发生偏转

If you are sailing in 'dirty wind' that has been deflected by someone else's sail, don't hesitate—tack and use the lift! Matters are much worse if you are in the dirty wind of several boats. This is the position when you are in the third rank at the start. It is essential that you get onto port tack and wriggle out, going under the starboard tack boats to the right-hand side of the course. Because of the turned wind from their sails you will be lifted or reaching, and hopefully eventually find some 'clean' air.

如果你的受风很差，正被其他船影响（风通过其船帆后发生偏转），千万不要犹豫——立刻迎风转向，转到上升舷航行！如果同时受好几条船影响，情况会更糟。这种情况通常发生在起航时第三排的位置。你必须左舷航行脱离出去，从右舷船下方穿过，来到航线右侧。

由于他们的帆会使风偏转，你将获得上升的风力或能够横风/后迎风航行，很有可能最终会找到一些清晰的风。

In team racing, when close covering, your aim is to get the opponent squarely in your backwind, tacking to keep covering him if he tacks. This will slow him down considerably, and he can be slowed even more if you oversheet as he loses speed. Don't slow down more than he does, or he will tack and go through you!

在团体赛中近距离遮挡时，你的目的是让对手正好处于你的尾风中。如果他迎风转向，你也转向来继续遮挡他。这会大大减慢他的速度。如果你在他减速时更多地收帆，他的速度会更慢。不要比他减速更多，否则他会迎风转向超过你！

When reaching, the deflected wind will make it difficult for anybody to pass close to leeward, as several boats in a group will produce a big block of slow-moving deflected wind.

侧顺风航行时，偏转的风会使任何人都难以从靠近下风侧的位置通过，因为聚集在一起的船只会形成一大片缓慢移动的风区。

On the run, an Optimist throws a disturbed wind area ahead of it. This goes for different distances ahead depending on the wind strength. Groups of running boats produce very damaging areas of slow-moving turbulent wind to be avoided at all costs by boats ahead and by boats on the beat—never beat through groups of running boats: even if you avoid the wind shadow, the wash will get you!

顺风航行时，OP 帆船的前方会形成一片扰动的风区，其范围取决于风力强度。大群顺风航行的船会形成移动缓慢且极具破坏性的乱风区，前方的船只和迎风船必须不惜一切代价避免进入该区域——切勿迎风航行穿过顺风船群：即使你避开了上风船的背风区，他们激起的浪花也会带来麻烦！

Wind Theory 风的相关理论

This is fascinating and essential knowledge for every sailor. Recommended reading is

Wind Strategy by David Houghton and Fiona Campbell—also part of Fernhurst Books' Sail to Win series—which covers the following vitally important concepts:

 对于每个水手来说，这都是极具吸引力且必不可少的知识。推荐阅读大卫·霍顿（David Houghton）和菲欧娜·坎贝尔（Fiona Campbell）撰写的《风的策略》（*Wind Strategy*）——也是 Fernhurst "航向胜利" 系列中的书籍。其中涵盖了以下一些极其重要的概念：

- Surface wind refraction
- 风在表面的偏移
- Stable and unstable air
- 稳定和不稳定的气流
- Coastal effects
- 海岸线影响
- Convergence and divergence
- 聚集和分散
- Typical lake winds
- 典型的湖风
- How tide and water temperature changes affect the wind
- 潮汐和水温变化对风的影响
- Gusts and lulls, downdrafts and squalls
- 阵风区和弱风区，下降气流和暴风雨
- Sea breezes
- 海风
- Messages from the clouds
- 不同云形代表的信息
- Obstacles in the wind
- 风中的障碍物

Windshift Sailing
运用风摆航行

 By keeping awake and using windshifts you can sail a shorter course upwind, covering the distance to the weather mark more directly and leaving those fast guys who went the wrong way struggling far astern!

 保持清醒，运用风摆，你就能缩短迎风航段，更直接地航行到上风标，让那些航行快速但是路线错误的水手望"船尾"兴叹。

Spotting Shifts 寻找风摆

- Watch your boat's heading on the shore ahead. When you are lifted you can point 'higher' up the shore; when backed 'lower'.
- 观察你的航向与前方海岸的关系。在受上升风摆时，能以高角度航行；在受逆时针风摆时，则能低角度航行。
- Be sensitive to the adjustments you have to make, feeling when you have been able to point higher or have had to bear away a lot to stay on the wind.
- 敏锐地调船，感受你什么时候能够更迎风，或者是否需要大幅度顺风偏转，以保持在风区内。
- Watch the boats around you. If you seem to be getting lifted above the boats to leeward and the boats to windward are being lifted above you, you are on a lift. If the boats to leeward of you suddenly seem to be pulling ahead and you are dropping down, while the boats to windward drop towards you, you are being headed!
- 注意周围的船只。如果你上升得高于下风船，你上风侧的船上升到高于你的位置，你就处于上升舷。如果你下风侧的船突然航行到你前面了，你在往下降，同时，你上风侧的船正往你这边下降，你就处于下降舷！
- Watch clouds, wind on the water, boats to windward.
- 观察云、水面上的风、上风侧的船。
- Use your compass.
- 使用指南针。

Getting To Know The Wind Pre-Start
在起航前熟悉风况

 You need to find out:
 明确以下细节：

- Wind shifts expected during the race, due to meteorological changes or sea breezes. The expected shifts can be worked out in advance from the weather forecast and inspired guesswork on the morning of the race.
- 由于气象变化或海风的影响，比赛期间会产生风摆。根据天气预报和比赛日早上的猜测，可以提前预测风摆。

CHAPTER 9 第九章　　Seeing The Wind 看　风

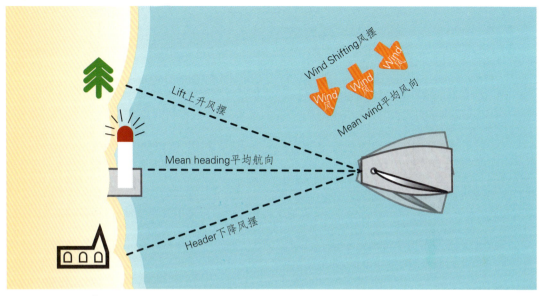

Watch your boat's heading when sailing towards the shore or a fixed object
在驶向岸边或某一固定目标物时，注意你的航向

- Wind bends on the course. Are these likely? Look at a map of the area. If you think there is a possibility of a wind bend, then agree with your buddy to check it with a split tack before the start.
- 风有可能在航线上偏转吗？查看比赛区域的地图，如果你觉得风可能会偏转，就和你的搭档一起在起航前从不同舷侧迎风转向，进行检查。
- When at the course, sail upwind and check the frequency of oscillation of the wind. Wind is seldom steady, oscillating from side to side with a frequency that may be as short as 30 seconds or as long as 30 minutes. By sailing the beat, you should get an idea of how many times you will have to tack to stay on the lifted tack.
- 在航线上迎风航行时，检查风摆的频率。风很少是稳定的，总是从一侧摆到另一侧，摆动频率短至 30 s，长达 30 min。通过航行迎风段，你大概能知道需要进行多少次迎风转向，使自己保持在上升舷。
- While you are doing this practice beat, try to find the mean wind direction and how large the shifts are. If you use a compass this will be a lot more precise. Look at the gusts and areas of stronger wind. Is there any pattern to them? Is there more wind in certain areas of the course or are gusts lifting more on one tack?
- 在进行尝试时，试着确定平均风向以及风摆的大小。使用指南针会更加精确。观察阵风区和强风区。它们是否有一定的规律？在航线上的某些区域是否风更多，或者阵风使得某一舷的上升风力更强？

Use The Compass 指南针的运用

Avoid using a compass until you are happy sailing an Optimist fast and accurately and you are comfortable sailing on shifts using feel, other boats and where you are heading on a shoreline. Once you reach this level of competence then a compass can be a valuable tool. Before that it can be a distraction.

刚开始应避免使用指南针，直到你能够快速准确地驾驶 OP 舒服地运用风摆航行，这需要借助你的感觉、其他船只以及你与海岸线的相对位置。一旦你达到这种水平，指南针就会成为一个非常有价值的工具。在此之前，它可能会分散你的注意力。

97

Once in the start area, sail upwind on one tack for ten minutes or so checking the frequency of oscillation and the maximum lift and maximum header. From these you can work out the mean wind direction and the compass settings / readings that represent the mean upwind course on each tack.

一旦到达起航区域，就选择在某一舷迎风航行 10 min 左右，检查风摆的频率以及最大上升风摆和最大下降风摆。从这些信息中，你可以得出平均风向和每一舷平均迎风航向的指南针读数。

The importance of this is that, when you are on a lift and the wind starts to back slowly, you must be careful not to tack until the wind and your upwind course have swung 'back' past the mean direction. In very shifty weather, if you lose sight of the mean headings on each tack you will be tacking on small headers and losing out badly.

这一点的重要性在于，当你处于上升舷，风缓慢地开始逆时针偏转时，注意一定不要迎风转向，直到风和你的迎风航向偏转超过平均风向。在很多风摆的情况下，如果你忽视了每一舷的平均航向，就会在一些较小的下降风摆下迎风转向，最后损失惨重。

After the start it is easy to glance at the compass to check that you are sailing on, or higher than, the mean upwind course for that tack without loss of concentration on speed. If you see that you are heading below the mean course, then take the first opportunity to tack! The result will be faultless shift sailing and a magnificent first mark position!

起航后，快速地瞥一眼指南针，确保你在这一舷的平均迎风航向上航行，或高于平均航向，同时保持船速。如果你发现自己低于平均航向，就抓住机会立刻迎风转向！从而完美地运用风摆，努力争取第一个绕标的位置。

Of course, it is not as easy as this. Not only are starboard tack boats preventing you from going where you want, but the wind itself does not always 'play the game'.

当然，实际操作并没有这么容易。不仅有右舷船会阻止你的去向，而且风也不一定能好好"配合"。

Don't Rely Only On The Compass
不要完全依靠指南针

Use your eyes as well. You can only depend on the compass for your tactics in winds that oscillate from a steady mean direction. Do not blindly sail on compass readings in the following circumstances:

运用双眼去观察。只有在平均风向稳定的风摆下，才可以完全依靠指南针制定应对风的

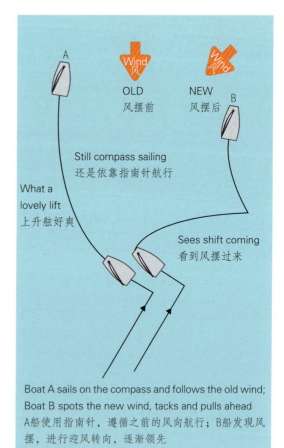

Boat A sails on the compass and follows the old wind; Boat B spots the new wind, tacks and pulls ahead
A船使用指南针，遵循之前的风向航行；B船发现风摆，进行迎风转向，逐渐领先

Don't rely only on the compass—get your head out of the boat and look for major changes to the wind
不要完全依靠指南针航行——注意观察船外的情形，寻找重大的风况变化

战术。在以下情况下，千万不要盲目地遵循指南针的读数航行：
- Wind bends on the course. (The compass may still be useful away from the influence of the bend.)
- 风在航线上偏转。（远离偏转的风影响，指南针可能仍然好用。）
- Meteorological changes in wind directions, such as a front crossing the race area or the sea breeze coming in. Such wind direction changes will make nonsense of mean wind estimates. If you do not spot that the wind is changing permanently, and take it to be just a good lift, you will end up sailing on a long, slowly lifting tack when it would have been better to take a short hitch towards the new wind direction and then lay the mark. Keep a good eye on boats to windward. What wind have they got? Where is it coming from? When the wind steadies again, by all means reset your compass but be cautious about trusting it absolutely.
- 气象变化改变风向，例如，风面穿过比赛区域或者有海风吹过来。这会让预测平均风向变得毫无意义。如果你没有及时发现风向已经完全改变，而认为这是一个很好的上升风摆，就会导致你在又长又缓慢的上升舷上耗费大量时间，而错过朝着改变后的风向短距离航行，快速来到方位线的机会。密切关注上风侧的船只，他们的受风如何？风是从哪儿来的？待风再次稳定时，务必重新设置指南针，但不要过于依赖。
- If the frequency of oscillation of the wind is longer than the duration of the windward leg, you will sail one beat on one part of the wind cycle and the next beat on another part. In these circumstances your compass is of little value except to give an idea of where you are in the cycle.
- 如果风摆的频率比迎风段的航行时间更长，你会在风摆循环周期的一个阶段内航行一个迎风段，在另一个阶段航行下一个迎风段。在这种情况下，指南针除了能让你知道你在周期中处于哪个阶段之外毫无价值。

CHAPTER 10 第十章

Understanding Current 理解涌流

A great number of venues you will race at will have current caused either by tide, river flow or the wind. This can be very confusing for sailors, especially if they normally sail inland.

大多数帆船比赛场地都会存在涌流，这些涌或许由于潮汐、河流或风的作用而产生。涌流可能带给水手们很大的困惑，尤其是平常在内陆学习帆船的水手。

The first thing to do is to research the venue. Is it likely to have current? Look on the internet to find tide tables. This will give you the high and low water times and the rise and fall of the water. Consider any river flows by looking at Google Maps. Or is it a big expanse of water that might have wind-driven current?

所以，首先要做的就是研究比赛场地，其是否可能存在涌流？上网查找相关的潮汐图表，你会获得高低水位发生的时间和高度信息。使用谷歌地图查询相关的河流情况。是否还有可能是因为风大而产生涌流？

Is the current likely to be the same across the whole of the course or is it likely to vary? If it is going to be different across the course, you may be able to use the current to your advantage or there might be only one way to go that will pay.

整个航线上的涌流都趋于一致吗？还是在不同的区域会有所变化？如果整个航线上的涌流是不同的，说不定可以加以运用，来提升自己的优势，有效的方法也许只有一种。

Current Uniform Across Course
涌流在航线上均匀分布

Let's assume the current is going to be uniform across the whole course for the race. This means that, as long as you stay inside the laylines upwind and sail a straight-line course between the marks downwind, you can concentrate on your normal wind and boat tactics—tacking on shifts, sailing into gusts and avoiding dirty air.

假设整个航线上的涌流是一致的，这就意味着在迎风航行时，你只要保持在方位线内侧，在上风标和下风标之间直线航行，充分运用正常风况的航行战术即可——遇阵风迎风转向，航行到阵风区以避免不清晰的受风。

This sounds easy but many sailors get this wrong and overstand marks, sail big loops down reaches and on the wrong gybe down the run.

这听起来好像很简单，但是很多水手都会犯这些错误：超过方位线，绕大圈侧顺风航行，顺风航行时在错误的一舷。

Let's think about the main factors to consider depending which way the current is flowing relative to the course / wind.

让我们根据涌流与航线/风的关系，思考一下应对涌流的关键点。

Wind Against Current 风与流相对
- Beware being over the start line. The current is pushing you over. Get a good transit and don't get on the line too early.
- 注意不要超过起航线，涌流会把你往前推。选择一个好的参考物，不要过早地来到起航线上。
- The beat will feel shorter and you will need to tack before the usual laylines as the current is pushing you up towards the windward

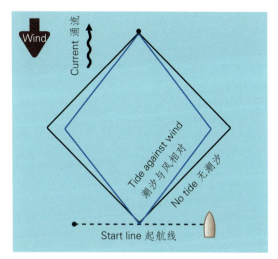

With wind against current, the beat will feel shorter and you need to tack earlier for the laylines

风与流相对时，你会感觉迎风段变短了，应早些迎风转向，来到方位线上

- mark.
- 你会感觉迎风段变短了，应在到达方位线之前迎风转向，因为涌流一直在将你往上风标的方向推。
- The waves will be steeper and closer together than normal. Be prepared to modify your technique to cope with this.
- 浪也显得更高，浪距也比平常更近。准备好调整自己的应对技巧。
- You can shoot the windward mark since the current is pushing you up, so a late tack in can be a good tactical move.
- 因为涌流一直在将你往上推，你可以选择在上风标旁快转绕标，因此晚些迎风转向绕标可能是很好的策略。
- The run will feel longer as you sail into the current and the fleet will be very close and bunch up as it rounds the windward mark. The big priority is to try to keep your air clear.
- 因为你在逆流航行，顺风段则会显得更长。整个船群会靠得很近，在绕上风标时，混战在一起。这时候，你的首要任务是尽力保持受风清晰。
- Make your turn late on the leeward marks since you will have to be careful not to get swept into them by the current.
- 在绕下风标时，晚些转向，要特别小心，避免被涌流推向浮标。
- Try not to get pushed high on the reach by the current else you will end up running into the mark with the tide against you. Not very fast! Use a front or back transit to sail the direct line. If there is no transit, look at both marks to make a judgement as to whether you are still sailing the direct route.
- 注意不要在侧顺风航行时被涌流往上风方向推，否则可能会导致你要逆流顺风驶向浮标。那你的船速肯定不会很快！在前方或后方选择一个参照物辅助直线航行。如果没有参照物，就通过观察上下风的浮标做出判断，确定你是否依旧直线航行。

Wind With Current 风与流同向

- The current is pushing you back from the start line. Get a good transit and don't get too far away from the line. You will have to keep sailing to stay on the line. There is often a big line sag in the middle of the line. The beat will feel longer, and you will need to overstand the normal laylines as the current is pushing you down.
- 涌流会把你从起航线往后推。找到一个好的参照物，不要离起航线太远。你要持续航行才能保持在起航线上。起航线的中间通常呈明显下凹状，迎风航段会感觉更长，你要航行超过平常的方位线，因为涌流一直在将你往下推。
- Beware of getting too close to the windward mark. The current is pushing you onto it. Never try to shoot the windward mark.
- 注意在绕上风标时，不要靠得太近。涌流会把你往浮标方向推。绝对不要在最后时刻突然迎风偏转绕标。
- The run will feel shorter as you sail with the current. This will mean that the fleet will spread out as it rounds the windward mark. Try to stay in the middle of the run else the current will sweep you past the mark and you will end up reaching to get to it.
- 你会感觉顺风段变短了，因为你在顺流航行。这意味着，船群会在绕上风标时分散开来。

在顺风航行时，试着保持在航线中间的位置，否则涌流会把你推过下风标，你就得迎风航行到达浮标了。

- Make your turn early on the leeward marks since you will have to be careful not to get swept past them by the current.
- 在下风标处早些转向，要特别小心涌流一下把你推过下风标。
- Try not to get pushed low on the reach by the current or else you will end up beating into the mark with the tide against you. Not very fast! Use a front or back transit to sail the direct line. If there is no transit, look at both marks to make a judgement as to whether you are still sailing the direct route.
- 注意不要在侧顺风航行时被涌流往下推，否则可能会导致你要逆迎风驶向浮标。那你的船速肯定不会很快！在前方或后方选择一个参照物辅助直线航行。如果没有参照物，就通过观察上下风的浮标做出判断，确定你是否依旧直线航行。

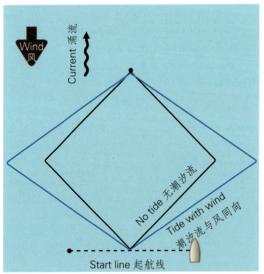

With wind with current, the beat will feel longer and you need to tack for the laylines later
风与流同向，你会感觉迎风段更长，应晚些迎风转向来到方位线

Current Across The Wind 风与流成直角

- The current will be pushing you towards one end of the start line. Beware of starting at the end the current is pushing to. It is very easy to get there too early, then you will end up in a raft on the pin or the committee boat.
- 水流会把你推向起航线的一端。注意不要从顺流的一端起航。很容易导致过早地来到起航线上，最后与起航线左侧标或组委会船发生碰撞。
- The beat will probably have a long and a short tack. Watch your laylines—one you will have to tack earlier on, the other you will need to overstand.
- 迎风段很可能由两段组成，一舷航行距离长，另一舷距离短。注意方位线——在一侧要尽早迎风转向来到线上，另一侧则需航行超过。
- Be aware of the current flow on the windward mark—it will either be pushing you hard onto it or sweeping you past it.
- 注意上风标处的水流——不是把你使劲往上风标推，就是把你推得过上风标。
- The run will have the tide across it, so it is likely to have a favoured gybe for the whole run. Try to get a transit on the leeward mark and sail a straight line to the mark.
- 顺风段受潮汐流影响，可能存在能够快速完成整个顺风段的有利一舷。试着找到一个下风标的参照物，直线航行到达。
- If the leeward mark is a gate think about which mark is better for the current. Will you get caught in a leebow from another boat when you round the mark or will the boat in front get swept wide and open up a lane for you?
- 如果下风标为门标，就要思考选择绕哪一边能够更好地利用水流。在绕标时，会被下风船影响吗？或是你前面的船会被水流冲到旁边，为你开道？
- The reach will either have the current behind you or you will be sailing into it. If sailing into it, this will close the fleet up and make the reach feel a lot longer. The opposite is true if the current is behind you.
- 侧顺风航行时，要么顺流，要么逆流。如果逆流，船群会非常接近，侧顺风段会更长；顺流的话，情况则相反。

CHAPTER 10 第十章　Understanding Current 理解涌流

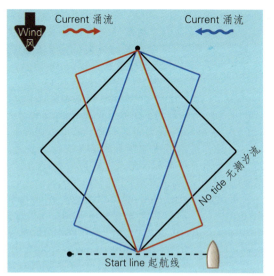

With wind across current, if the windward mark is laid directly upwind, one tack will be longer
风与流成直角，如果上风标完全迎风，有一舷的航行时间会更长

Current Varying Across The Course
航线上变化的涌流

The current can vary in strength or direction across the course. If this is the case, the important factor is to ensure you sail in the least adverse current or the strongest advantageous current.

在航线不同位置的涌流流速或方向可能会有所不同。如果是这样，那么一定确保在不利水流最弱或有利水流最强的区域航行。

How can you predict where the current is strongest or where the direction might change?
如何预测哪里的水流最强，或者在哪里水流会改变方向？

Venturi Effect 文丘里效应

This is the effect where the flow of water increases as it is squeezed or compressed through a gap such as between a shoreline and an island.

这一效应指的是，水流在通过间隙（例如海岸线和一个海岛）时被挤压或压缩，流速增大。

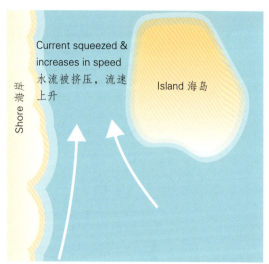

If the current is squeezed into a gap, it will get faster
如果水流被挤压进一个空隙，流速将上升

It could be that it is just compressed trying to get around a headland. Remember this will also cause a change in direction of the flow. In extreme circumstances a headland can cause the flow to sweep around it and then swirl into a reversed flow (a back eddy).

具体情况可能是，水流在绕过海岬时被挤压，流速上升。记住，水流的方向也会因此改变。在极端情况下，水流在绕过海岬后发生旋转，逆向流动（逆涡流）。

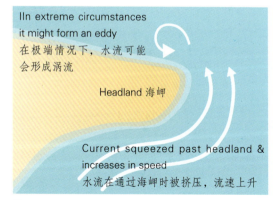

The current can be compressed going around a headland—which will also change its direction and possibly cause eddies
水流在绕过海岬时被挤压，流速上升——同时改变流向，可能会形成涡流

103

Shallow Water 浅水区

Current flows slower in shallow water because of the friction with the sea or riverbed. So, if current is flowing along the shoreline, it is likely to be slower inshore and faster out to sea.

由于与海床或河床的摩擦，水流在浅水区的流速会变慢。所以，如果水流沿着海岸线流动，近岸区域流速慢，越往海深处，流速越快。

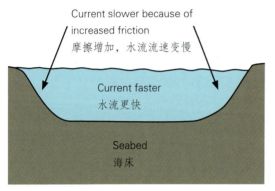

The current flows slower in shallow water
水流在浅水区流速慢

However, if a current is passing over a shallow bank it will speed up because of the Venturi effect mentioned above. So be careful, not all shallow water is slower moving!

当水流在通过浅滩时，由于上文所述的"文丘里"效应，流速会上升。所以，要注意，浅水区并不意味着水流缓慢！

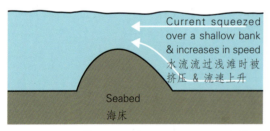

The Venturi effect can happen over a shallow bank, increasing the speed of the current
文丘里效应可能会发生在浅滩上，使水流流速上升

Bends Around Land 绕过陆地

Current will try to take the easiest route around shorelines or islands. This will bend the current direction and might mean the current is different at the top of the course to the bottom.

水流在通过海岸线或海岛时，会选择最简单的路线。这会改变水流的方向，可能导致航线顶部和底部的水流出现差异。

Once you have predicted how the current will be flowing on the course it is important that you check exactly what it is doing on the course.

一旦你对水流在航线上的情况进行了预测，务必检查水流的实际动向。

A good visual clue as to changes in current strength or direction are tide lines. Where different current flows meet you will probably see either a disturbance in the wave pattern, a difference in water colour or maybe a line of seaweed or rubbish floating in the water.

潮汐线是一个很好的视觉线索，你会观察到水流流速或方向的变化。如果不同方向的水流相遇，你很可能会看到它们的波形出现干扰，水色不同，或者水中漂浮着一行海草或垃圾。

To tell the direction and strength of the current look at any fixed objects such as a mark, lobster pot or the anchored committee boat. Look at how the water is flowing around it.

通过观察固定的物体，例如浮标、虾笼或抛锚的组委会船，判断水流的方向和速度。观察水是如何围绕目标物流动的。

To be more accurate use a sponge or an almost full water bottle and throw it into the water next to the object. How far does it drift in one minute and in what direction? Don't forget to retrieve your bottle or sponge!

为了更准确地判断，可使用一块海绵或一个装满水的瓶子，将其扔到一个固定物体旁。观察它在一分钟内漂了多远，往什么方向？当然，最后别忘了收回瓶子或海绵。

This is where your coach can also be useful. They should have a tide stick so they can get readings around the course and feed them back to you before the start. This will help you make the best strategic and tactical decisions about the current.

这种时候你的教练也可以提供帮助。他们应该配备有一个潮汐测量棒，在航线上获取潮汐数据，并在起航前反馈给你。这能帮助你做出最佳的策略和战术决策，以应对水流的影响。

You can see the direction and strength of the current against a buoy
你可以通过观察浮标来判断涌流的方向和大小

A change in the water surface can show a change in the current
水面的变化意味着涌流的变化

MIND & BODY
精神 & 身体

PART 5　第五部分

CHAPTER 11 第十一章
Mental Fitness 心理健康

In the top of any national squad you tend to find accomplished and experienced sailors who have good boat handling skills, knowledge of tactics and the racing rules, race-prepared boats with good sails, and the ability to sail fast.

顶尖的帆船国家队中，你会发现颇有成就、经验丰富的水手通常都善于控船，对于战术和比赛规则有充分的认识，配有装配优质的比赛用船，具备快速航行的能力。

Why is it, then, that certain people win nearly all the time?

那么，为什么有的人几乎总是能赢？

Why Some People Win 获胜的原因

Objective Evaluation 评估目标

Winners are able to evaluate their own feelings and performance before, during and after competition. They develop the ability to examine their performance, identify strong and weak points (through using approaches described in this chapter), and then use that knowledge to plan changes in tactics or training to correct matters. They are also capable of identifying damaging emotions before, during or after a competition. They have a 'growth mindset' attitude.

获胜者能够在赛前、赛中和赛后评估自己的感受和表现。他们培养了检查自我表现、明确自身优缺点的能力（通过本章所述的方法），然后运用这些信息，改善自己的战术或培训，纠正自己的问题。他们还能够在赛前、赛中或赛后识别自己的不良情绪。他们通常具备"成长型心态"。

Clear Planning 计划清晰

Winners are able to set achievable training goals covering specific processes which require work (e.g. bailing to windward). They set performance goals (e.g. sail the beat perfectly; plan tactics for every situation), and also set outcome goals (e.g. win a race in the Nationals, top ten in the Worlds).

获胜者能够给自己设定可实现的训练目标，着重培训特定的操作流程（例如在迎风航行时排水）。他们会设置绩效目标（例如完美地航行迎风段；针对每种情况制定战术），同样也给自己设置结果目标（例如在全国比赛中赢得一轮比赛，在世锦赛中排名前十）。

Highly Confident 高度自信

Winners are totally confident of their ability. They are sure they can sail a perfect race, and winning or not winning is subject only to the vagaries of the sport. They have perfected techniques to maintain their confidence and block out failures.

获胜者对于自己的能力充满信心。他们确信自己能够在比赛中完美地航行，输赢完全取决于这项运动的变化莫测。他们拥有保持自信、避免失败的完美技巧。

Stress Management 压力管理

Winners are aware of their levels of stress and can use techniques to keep that level optimum for top performance. If you are too stressed, or too laid-back, performance suffers.

获胜者能够意识到自己的压力等级，并运用合理的技巧将其控制在适当程度，以在比赛中输出最佳表现。如果压力过大或过低，都会影响比赛的发挥。

Mental Rehearsal 心理排练

Winners are able to visualise their sailing so effectively that they can practise starts, mark roundings and other tactical manoeuvres without going afloat.

获胜者能够高效地想象自己航行的画面，使他们可以在完全不下水的情况下，在头脑中练习起航、绕标和其他战术操作。

Visualise surfing down a wave so you get it right on the water
想象自己滑浪的操作，这样真正下水的时候，你就能做到了

Winners have a developed ability to visualise each different part of the race, to examine it and the emotions felt at that time. You can use visualisation techniques to come to terms with a race in which you made a major error by visualising a successful outcome. If you lost your cool at a particular time in a race, you could visualise the lead-up to the incident, trying to pinpoint exactly what threw you.

获胜者培养发达的想象力，能够想象比赛中的不同环节，以进行检查，并且感受自己当时的情绪。你可以运用想象技巧处理一场出现重大失误的比赛，想象自己最终依旧取得了胜利。如果你在比赛中的某个时刻失去了冷静，就回想在此之前的场景，试着准确地找出你崩溃的原因。

Concentration 专注力

Winners have developed the ability to concentrate deeply for long periods.

获胜者培养了长时间保持深度专注的能力。

In addition, a characteristic of Olympic competitors is their strong will to win. To excel at that standard of competition, strong motivation is essential. These competitors have the overpowering ambition to be 'better than all the rest'. They don't want to lose, but must avoid the negative fear of losing. This drives them to try harder, hike further and longer, concentrate more, sail accurately and carefully, think fast, keep mentally calm, stay physically flexible, and work!

除此以外，奥运选手的一个共有特质是求胜心强。要想在竞争中脱颖而出，强大的动力必不可少。这些竞争者都有着无法压倒的雄心，"要比其他人都强"。他们不想输，但是也必须克服对输的恐惧。这驱使他们更努力地尝试，压舷更靠外，时间更久，更专注。小心准确地航行，快速思考，保持冷静，肢体灵活，不断努力！

Winners are driven to try harder, hike further and longer and concentrate more
获胜者会更努力尝试，压舷更靠外，时间更久，更专注

Mental Tools
心理工具

Training & Racing Log 培训 & 比赛日记

As an aid to self-coaching, on the evening after a race day, thoughtfully and honestly fill in a Race Analysis Sheet (p116).

运用竞赛分析表（第151页）辅助自学，在比赛结束当晚认真诚实地进行填写。

The most important entries will not be mast rake, sail used or foil rake, but your assessment of your performance. What went well and what aspects of your sailing need more work?

分析表中最重要的事项不是桅杆倾度、所用船帆或是稳向板倾斜度，而是你对自己表现的评估：哪些方面做得很好，哪些方面需要更多的努力和改进？

The next step is to do something about it! Keep these sheets in your log and, as you achieve your training and medium term goals, your confidence will improve with your results.

接下来要做的就是，采取行动！将这些表格保存在你的航行日记中，随着你逐步实现各种培训和中期目标，你的自信心也会随之提高。

Scrapbook 剪贴簿

Keep this for results, pictures, sailing instructions and so on and, when you've had a bad day, thumb through and see how much you have improved and remember your good races.

剪贴簿用于保存你的比赛成绩、照片和航行细则等。在表现不佳的时候，拿出来浏览一下，看自己进步了多少，回顾自己表现良好的时候。

Keep a log of your performances
记录自己的表现

Keep a 'scalp' page and enter the name of every top sailor you beat. If you can beat them once you can do it again! Keep notes of anything you learnt or interesting information.

单独用一页记录每一个你打败的水手的名字。如果你曾经战胜过他们一次，那么你一定可以再次打败他们！同时，记下你所学的所有内容或者有趣的信息。

Video 视频

If you've had a good race or series, try to get a copy of a video of it. Every time you watch it you will get a confidence boost. It will also help you visualise yourself sailing well.

如果你在某场比赛或系列赛的成绩非常好，试着找到比赛视频并保存下来。每次观看这些视频都会增强你的信心。而且这些视频还能帮助你更好地想象自己过往的出色表现。

Talk 沟通

Take every chance to talk to top sailors about how they've achieved their successes, and imagine yourself in their shoes.

抓住每个和顶尖水手沟通的机会，问问他们是如何成功的，设身处地地想象自己处于他们的位置。

"30 Second Bubble" "30 秒泡泡"

This is a useful way of coping with things that happen during a race. Shut out anything that has happened over 30 seconds ago. Concentrate only on the present and immediate future as if you are in a bubble of time.

这种方法对于应对实际赛场非常有用。具体做法是：忘掉30秒前发生的一切。只专注于眼前和即将发生的未来，就像你置身于一个时间泡泡中一样。

The bubble will help you exclude from your mind everything that has or will happen outside that time. Forget the hassle; let it go, settle down, control yourself and get back to concentrating on simply sailing fast!

这个泡泡会帮助你从脑海中排除那段时间之外已经发生或将要发生的一切。忘掉问题；放下情绪，冷静下来，把控好自己，重新专注于快速航行！

Look Forward & Out 往前看 & 往外看

This is another useful coping technique. If something happens, try to forget it by concentrating hard on sailing your boat fast purely by feel, keeping your eyes forward and out, scanning only the water immediately ahead and to leeward until you have control again.

这是另一个好用的比赛应对技巧。如有情况发生，试着转移注意力，努力凭感觉使自己的船快速航行，注意观察前面和船外的情形，审视前方水域和下风情况，直到你再次冷静下来。

If something goes wrong, look forward and out
如果出问题了，就往前看，往外看

Examine Your Emotions 情绪自查

An example is fear. What are you afraid of exactly? Is it a logically justified fear? Is it stiffening your muscles or interfering with your breathing? Fear is a natural safety mechanism, making you 'freeze'.

例如，恐惧。你到底在害怕什么？这种恐惧合乎逻辑吗？它是否使你肌肉僵硬或者影响了你的呼吸？恐惧是一种自然的安全生理机制，它会使你"无法动弹"。

It's natural; you can't do anything about it; so accept it but be firm that you are not going to let it rule you or interfere with your race.

这是一种自然反应，你无法改变；那就接受它，但是要坚定地表明：你不会让恐惧主宰你或干扰你的比赛。

Desensitisation To Aggravating Factors 放大脱敏法

If you get up-tight when people shout, get all the other members of your training group to shout during exercises. After coping with friendly shouting, strangers shouting in competition will not be so daunting.

如果你在他人喊叫时会感到非常紧张，就在训练时，让队里的所有成员都大喊大叫。在你经历过友好的喊叫后，面对比赛中陌生人的喊叫就不会觉得战战兢兢。

Similarly, competitors have to learn to accept decisions of 'on the water judges', however inept or wrong they may seem at the time. This can be practised by introducing a number of unjust and erroneous rulings into training that competitors have to accept.

同样，选手们必须学会接受裁判在水上的判决，无论当时看起来多么不合理或错误。练习方法是，在训练中引入一些不公平或错误的判决，让选手们不得不接受。

Self-Affirmation & Buzz Words 自我肯定 & 鼓励用语

Look in the mirror on race day, look yourself in the eye, and say 'You're good—you've beaten them all before'. Say 'Great!' when things go right, 'Good tack!' when you do a good one, 'Slippery!' as you slide swiftly downwind. When you pull off a cunning move, say 'Sneaky!', 'Another one bites the dust!', or something similar. It will keep you hyped up and flying. Build up a selection of buzz words to use at different times in the race.

在比赛日当天对着镜子，看着自己的眼睛说："你很棒——你曾经打败过他们所有人。"在进展顺利时，对自己说"太好了！"；在迎风转向做得很好时，说"转得漂亮！"；在顺风快速滑行时,说"滑得好!";在你计谋得逞的时候,说"真是机智!""又干掉一个!"或类似的话。这些话能让你保持情绪高涨,快速航行。组织一系列的鼓励话语,用于比赛的不同时刻。

Arousal 保持觉醒

If you are feeling lethargic after a postponement or waiting around between starts, force yourself to begin checking the wind and your boat set-up, and practise some boat handling. This should get you more focussed.

如果比赛延迟或在等待起航信号时,你感到昏昏沉沉,就强迫自己检查一下风况和船只设置,并做一些控船练习。这一系列操作应能让你重新专注起来。

Controlled Aggression 有控制地进攻

This can be effective afloat in getting your own way. In using this technique, it is essential that you can keep your mind cool and clear, and do not infringe the rules. Be very careful that you do not show bad sportsmanship and unfair sailing (RRS 2) or 'commit an act of misconduct' (RRS 69). This clearly excludes the use of bad language and bullying in your dealings with other competitors.

这种方式能让你在水上有效地达成自己的目标。在使用此技巧时,必须保持头脑冷静、思维清醒,不要违反规则。切勿做出有违体育道德和公平航行(《帆船竞赛规则》第2条)或"品行不端"(《帆船竞赛规则》第69条)的行为。这明确了,在与竞争对抗衡时,使用脏话和欺凌他人都是不被允许的。

Assertiveness 自信果敢

Sailors need to develop assertiveness, based on a sound knowledge of the rules. A loud and clear early hail of 'Protest' can work wonders. Don't let the aggressive kids have it all their own way!

水手们要在充分了解规则的基础上,培养自己自信果敢的品质。在必要时,尽早大声响亮地喊出"抗议"会有奇效。不要让那些咄咄逼人的对手们称心如意!

Singing & Whistling 唱歌 & 吹口哨

These are good for you when racing. They help you relax and distract the opposition. The secret is to develop the ability to do them without thinking about it!

这些技巧对比赛会有所帮助。它们可以使你放松下来,并分散对手的注意力。秘诀在于,努力发展这些能力,直到你能够不假思索地运用它们。

Executioner's Eye, Gunslinger's Smile 志在必得,泰然自若

This is a phrase from a book by Dennis Conner who won the America's Cup four times. It is useful when in tactical battles with an opponent. It is also handy in helping you counter the psyching-out and winding-up talk that goes on in the dinghy park at big events.

这句话(Executioner's Eye, Gunslinger's Smile)出自丹尼斯·康纳(Dennis Conner)所著的一本书,他曾四次获得美洲杯帆船赛的冠军。该技巧在与对手进行战术对抗的时候非常有用。还能在大型比赛中帮你应对各种扰乱心绪和挑衅的对话,例如在赛场停船区遇到一些出言不逊的人。

If somebody is trying to get you worried, give him the gunslinger's smile and look him over for execution!

如果有人试图扰乱你的心态,泰然自然地朝他微微一笑,表明"咱们水上见真招"!

Ten Things That Require Zero Talent 凡人十事

While much of this book is about the skills and techniques which determine your sailing talent, there are a lot of things which can help your sailing which require no talent—just the right attitude. Here are the commonly quoted top ten:

虽然本书讲述了大量决定个人航海才能的技术技巧,但还有很多其他方面有助于你的航行,无须天赋——只要你有正确的态度。以下是最常说到的十个品质:

CHAPTER 11 第十一章　　Mental Fitness 心理健康

1. Punctuality
1. 守时
2. Work ethic
2. 职业道德
3. Effort
3. 努力
4. Body language
4. 肢体语言
5. Energy
5. 精力

6. Attitude
6. 态度
7. Passion
7. 热情
8. Being coachable
8. 接受指导
9. Doing extra
9. 额外付出
10. Being prepared
10. 做好准备

Have these attitudes and your sailing talent will go further!
拥有这样的态度，你将能更好地发展自己的航海才能！

Be assertive, particularly in close situations
保持自信果敢，尤其是在近距离对抗时

113

CHAPTER 12 第十二章
The Perfect Body 完美体格

Heavy Or Lightweight?
重了还是轻了？

Weight is of great interest to Optimist sailors and their parents! Usually they have no need to worry, for the Optimist is a remarkably weight-tolerant boat. An experienced heavyweight can confound opinion and turn in winning performances in all weathers. A demonstration of this was given by Ben Ainslie at the 1992 UK National Championship, which he dominated in both light and heavy weather, weighing 63kg (10 stone). Although this was a long time ago, and it was Ben, it is still applicable.

OP水手和其父母们十分重视体重问题！通常不用太担心，因为OP帆船对于体重的兼容度相当高。经验丰富、体重较重的水手更是能打破常规观念，在各种天气下表现出色。1992年本·安斯利（Ben Ainslie）在英国锦标赛上的表现就是很好的说明，他在小风和大风情况下均占主导地位，而他当时的体重是63 kg（10英石）。虽然这件事情发生在很久以前，而且你可能觉得本·安斯利的例子有些特殊，但这个观点依旧适用。

For average sailing conditions the optimum sailing weight would probably be 35–56kg (6–8st), but each weight group has its own particular problems of rig tune, trim, movement in the boat and technique which have to be solved for top performance.

对于一般的航行条件来说，水手的最佳体重量应为35~56 kg（6~8英石），但是每个重量群体都有一些特定的技术问题需要解决，如调船、调帆、在船内的移动和技巧，才能获得最佳表现。

The Optimist can be sailed by lightweights and heavyweights
体重较轻和较重的水手均能驾驶OP

Physical Development
发展体能

Optimist sailing spans late childhood and early adolescence. During this time the steady growth of childhood leads into the 'growth spurt', a two-year period of very rapid height gain, after which growth slows down as adult height is reached. Individuals develop at very different rates: early developers may be physically up to four years ahead of their peers in height and strength, but their growth stops earlier. By 18 they have often been passed by guys who were the smallest in the class at the age of 12!

OP 航海的年龄段跨越童年晚期和青春期早期。在此期间，宝宝从稳定增长的儿童期逐渐进入为期两年的"快速生长期"，身高快速增长，之后随着孩子达到成年身高，成长速度逐渐减缓。每个人的发育速度有很大不同：早发育者的身高和力量可能会比同龄人超前四年，但他们的生长也会更早停止。到了 18 岁，当初 12 岁时班里最瘦小的孩子都可能超过他们。

In the Optimist class it is common to see these well-co-ordinated and strong early developers dominating the younger age groups, but they can get too big and heavy in their final Optimist year. By this time their later-maturing friends are getting stronger and are reaching optimum weight.

在 OP 级别中，我们经常可以看到一些肢体协调、身体强壮的早发育的孩子在年龄较小的群体中名列前茅。但是在他们 OP 航海的最后一年，可能会出现体格过大、过重的现象。到那个时候，在同龄人中晚熟的一些朋友则变得越来越强壮，达到 OP 航行的最佳体重。

Growth Risks 成长风险

Identifying the growth spurt is important because, during this time, the mechanical advantage of muscle groups change, making an individual much more susceptible to injury. This problem can be seen most clearly in some thin children who go through an awkward clumsy phase during their growth spurt, when the bones seem to grow faster than the muscle needed to move them and the nervous system's ability to control them.

识别快速生长期很重要，因为在此期间，肌肉群的力学优势会发生变化，个体会更容易受伤。这样的问题在一些瘦弱的孩子身上尤为明显，他们在快速生长期显得十分笨拙。因为他们骨骼的生长速度似乎快于肌肉生长的速度和神经系统对其进行控制的能力。

All young athletes in training are particularly at risk of sustaining injury to the growing bone ends, ligaments and muscles when exercising strenuously. The most common and well-known problem for sailors (as for footballers) is Osgood Schlatter's Syndrome, a painful swelling on the upper end of the tibia where the patella tendon attaches to the growing area of bone. Hiking hard (or kicking a heavy football) can lead to strain and considerable inflammation at this point, as the muscular action of the quadriceps tries to pull the tendon off the bone. The treatment is rest and no hiking (or kicking) until it settles, sometimes for six months!

所有处于训练中的年轻运动员在剧烈运动时，都特别容易对生长中的骨骼末端、韧带和肌肉造成损伤。众所周知，水手（像足球运动员一样）最常见的问题就是奥斯古德－施拉特症候群（又称胫骨结节骨骺炎），即在胫骨上端与髌骨肌腱附着的生长区域发生疼痛性肿胀。剧烈压舷（类似踢一个很重的足球）会导致此处产生拉伤和严重的炎症，因为股四头肌的肌力会迫使髌腱与胫骨分离。治疗方法就是休息，不要压舷（或踢球）直到症状缓解，有时需要长达六个月的时间！

Boys & Girls 男孩 & 女孩

Adolescence in boys brings a sharp increase in height, weight, shoulder width, muscle, bone mass and strength. They become leaner, losing the body fat of childhood. Boys have the peak of their growth spurt around about the age of 14, but it can be as early as 12 or as late as 16. Adult height is usually reached at about 17 or 18.

青春期的男孩会在身高、体重、肩宽、肌肉、骨量和力量上急剧增长。他们会变得更加瘦削，失去童年时期的体脂。男生的生长突增大约在14岁左右，早至12岁，晚至16岁。通常在17或18岁左右达到成年身高。

In girls, adolescence brings first an increase in height, followed some six months later by a weight increase. Their strength does increase at this time, but much less than the boys and most of the weight gain is in fat rather than muscle. Girls have their growth spurt peak around the age of 12, though it may be as early as 10 or as late as 14. By 15 to 16 a girl will normally have reached full adult height.

对于女孩来说，进入青春期后首先会出现身高增长，大约六个月后体重也会增加。在此期间，她们的力量也会增加，但是会比男孩小得多，而且体重增加的大部分是脂肪而不是肌肉。女生的生长高峰期在12岁左右，早至10岁，晚至14岁。通常在15至16岁达到成年身高。

In the final Opi year (aged 15) girls have had their growth spurt and strength gain, without the full weight gain of late teen years. Boys on the other hand are in the middle of their growth and have not yet developed the muscle of later years. It is thus still possible for boys and girls to compete equally.

在OP航海的最后一年（15岁），女生们会经历快速生长期，力量增加，但是体重不会像青春期后期那样全面增长。另一方面，男生正处于生长中期，肌肉尚未发育完全。因此，男孩和女孩仍能平等竞争。

Puberty and an increase in hormone levels can cause physical, mood and behavioural changes in adolescent children as well as mental and emotional preoccupation. The onset of menstruation must be treated sympathetically, but it need not necessarily affect performance in training and competition.

青春期以及荷尔蒙水平的上升会导致青春期儿童的身体、情绪和行为发生变化，以及精神和情绪上的专注度变化。女生经期来时必须要注意照顾她们的情绪，但是并不一定会影响训练和比赛成绩。

Boys and girls can compete against each other in Optimists
男生和女生驾驶OP在比赛中相互竞争

CHAPTER 13 第十三章
Physical Fitness 体 能

Physical fitness is seldom necessary for successful performance at club level, but becomes increasingly important for good results at regional, national and international levels.

通常想要在俱乐部级别的比赛中有出色表现,体能不是必要条件,但是想要在区域、全国和国际级别的比赛中取得好成绩,体能就显得越发重要。

Fitness Helps
体能的效用

Fitness can help your sailing in four main ways:

体能主要在四个方面有助于航行:

1. It helps to prevent you from getting tired. Racing, particularly in heavy weather, can be exhausting. If you are fit, you will be able to sail harder and keep fighting longer than the next sailor. This will have you moving up the leaderboard.
   防止疲劳。竞赛可能会使人精疲力竭,尤其是在恶劣天气情况下。如果你的体能很好,就能比其他水手更努力地航行,奋战更持久。最终在排行榜上名列前茅。

2. It speeds up your recovery between races. The demands of championship sailing are often much greater than those encountered in a single event. Incomplete recovery between races held 'back to back' or on successive days can lead to you getting more and more tired, and less capable of doing your best in the races at the end of a hard series. Avoid this by being physically fit.
   加快选手在比赛间的恢复。锦标赛对水手的体能要求通常比其他单次赛事更高。在持续比赛或连续比赛日中间恢复不全可能会导致你越来越疲惫,并且在艰难的系列赛后期无法发挥出最佳水平。可通过保持良好的体能来避免这一问题。

3. It keeps you sharp mentally. Tired, unfit sailors find concentration difficult. This affects their ability to make quick correct tactical decisions, and their performance suffers. Physical exhaustion makes it much harder to keep mentally positive and cope emotionally with events during the race. The fitter you are the better you will perform mentally.
   保持思维敏捷。疲劳不堪、体能欠佳的水手很难集中注意力,这会使他们无法快速做出正确的战术决策,从而影响他们的表现。身体的疲惫使得他们难以在比赛中保持良好的精神状态,并处理好自己的情绪。体能越好,精神状态就越好。

4. It prevents injuries. Most injuries occur when the body is tired and cold. When you are fit, you are much less likely to injure yourself when racing hard. Minimise injuries by being fit and more able to withstand what competing throws at you.
   防止受伤。大多数的身体损伤都是在疲劳或寒冷时发生的。如果你的体能足够好,在激烈的比赛中受伤的可能性就会大大降低。保持良好的体能,最大限度地降低受伤的可能性,你就能更好地承受竞争给你带来的冲击。

Training Requirements
培训要求

Size & Weight 体格 & 体重

Training requirements vary with a

competitor's size. Sailors weighing less than 35kg should aim to develop stamina, hiking and arm strength. Sailors weighing over 50kg need to develop flexibility, agility, balance and coordination, although stamina is still needed in heavy weather.

培训要求根据选手的体格而有差异。体重低于 35 kg 的水手，应努力发展耐力、压舷和手臂力量。体重超过 50 kg 的水手，则需培养柔韧性、敏捷性、平衡性和协调性。当然，在恶劣天气下还是需要耐力的。

Time On The Water 水上时间

Hours on the water can, of course, make a useful contribution to fitness. If you could sail three times a week for an hour or more in winds of force 4 or above, you would certainly develop good sailing fitness. However, it is impractical for most Optimist sailors to do this even if the wind were suitable. In the summer only 30% of days in Britain have winds of this strength or more. More winter days have suitable winds but, with a winter race training programme, extra stamina and fitness training is needed. This can be provided by sport and fun in and out of school:

无须赘言，数小时的水上训练对体能会很有帮助。如果你每周能在四级或以上风力下航行 3 次，每次持续一小时或更长的时间，你肯定能锻炼出很好的航海体能。不过即便风况适宜，这对于大多数 OP 水手来说也有些不切实际。因为在英国的夏季，只有 30% 的时间有这种强度或更强的风。更多时候，冬天的风会很合适，但是，要进行冬季比赛训练项目，就需要额外的耐力和体能训练。可结合校内外的运动和娱乐活动来培养：

- Flexibility: Stretching and warm-up exercises
- 柔韧性：拉伸和热身练习
- Balance: Surfing; windsurfing; skateboarding; wiggle boarding
- 平衡性：冲浪、帆板、滑板、摇摆滑板
- Agility: Football; rugby; hockey; netball
- 敏捷性：足球、橄榄球、曲棍球、投球
- Co-ordination and reactions: Badminton; table tennis; tennis; squash; golf
- 协调性和反应力：羽毛球、乒乓球、网球、壁球、高尔夫球
- Strength: Circuits or rugby training
- 力量：循环训练或橄榄球训练
- Stamina: Distance running; jogging; cycling; swimming
- 耐力：长跑、慢跑、骑自行车、游泳

Warm-Up & Flexibility
热身 & 柔韧性

Warming-Up 热身

Warming-up before training and exercise avoids injuring cold muscles and ligaments. Ideally you should warm-up and warm-down before and after all strenuous sailing. Before races it is often worth warming-up twice—on shore and just after the orange flag is displayed. After general recalls or a postponement a warm-up routine can not only help the muscles but will also help to wake you up and get you ready to fight.

在训练和运动前热身，能避免因为肌肉发冷而受伤或韧带拉伤。理想情况下，应在剧烈的航海训练前后进行热身和放松。通常在比赛前，很有必要进行两次热身——岸上一次，橙色信号旗升起后一次。在集体召回或比赛推迟后，热身不仅对肌肉很有帮助，还能使你保持清醒，准备好开始奋战。

Flexibility 柔韧性

This refers to the range of movement which is possible at joints. You need a fair amount of flexibility to move around a boat smoothly and easily. Some girls have most amazing natural flexibility, while some boys, particularly the muscular early developers, can be remarkably stiff.

柔韧性指关节的活动幅度。在船上灵活自如地移动需要相当程度的柔韧性。有些女生天生就具有令人惊叹的柔韧性，而有些男生则十分僵硬，尤其是肌肉发育早的。

Flexibility can be improved by regular gentle stretching exercises. For these to be effective, the end of the range of movement must be reached and the position held for a few seconds. It is important that such exercises are always carried out in a controlled manner. Violent, rapid or bouncing movements should be avoided as these are likely to be ineffective and may lead to injury.

定期开展一些柔和的拉伸练习能提高柔韧性。为了达到效果，在最大限度地拉伸后，保持姿势几秒钟。很重要的一点是，在练习时要有条不紊地控制自己的动作。避免剧烈、快速或弹跳的动作，因为这些动作很可能无法起到锻炼的目的，反而导致受伤。

First Warm-Up: Flexibility 首次热身：柔韧性

1. Running on the spot: 1 minute; or Step-ups: 15 leading with right leg, 15 with left
1. 原地跑: 1 min, 或上下台阶: 右腿为主上下15次, 再以左腿为主上下15次

2. Arm circling: 15 forward, 15 back
2. 双臂绕圈：往前15次，往后15次

3. Back flexion stretch: Lying on back with knees bent; draw right knee and nose together using hands to help: repeat with left knee, then both knees
3. 曲背拉伸：仰卧，屈膝，双手抬右腿辅助，将右膝往鼻子方向靠拢：之后换左膝，然后双膝同时靠拢

4. Quadriceps stretch: Lie on front, bend left knee; reach behind with the left hand, hold left foot, bring it to buttock, and increase stretch so that knee just rises from floor: repeat with right
4. 股四头肌拉伸：俯卧，曲左膝；左手向后伸，握住左脚，将其靠近臀部，增强拉伸程度，使膝盖刚好离开地板：换右脚重复上述动作

5. Shoulder stretch: Standing feet astride, hands in front of chest, arms horizontal, press elbows backwards then forwards

5. 肩部拉伸：双脚分开站立，双手置于胸前，双臂水平，向后推肘，然后向前

6. Trunk twist with head turning: Start as for shoulder stretch; rotate trunk and head to left; repeat to right

6. 扭头转体：从肩部拉伸的起始姿势开始，向左旋转躯干和头部，然后向右重复该动作

7. Side bend: Standing, feet shoulder-width apart, press one hand on hip while stretching the opposite arm over the head at 45°: repeat other side

7. 侧身上举：站立，双脚分开与肩同宽，一只手按在臀部上，同时另一只手臂在头顶上方呈 45° 伸展；换另一侧重复该动作

8. Sitting stretch: Sitting with both legs outstretched, gradually lean forwards from the hips—do not push towards the feet by rounding the back and leading with the head, as this can cause back strain

8. 坐姿伸展：双腿伸直坐着，从髋部开始逐渐前倾——不要弓背和伸头去够脚部，这很容导致背部拉伤

9. Back extension stretch: Lie on the floor face down with hands palm down under the shoulders, and forearms alongside trunk; push up the trunk keeping the hips on the floor; relax in this position, then slowly lower

9. 背部伸展：俯卧，双手掌心朝下置于肩下，前臂与躯干并列；向上推躯干，保持髋部接触地板；保持该姿势放松一会，然后慢慢放下

Warming Up Afloat 水上热身

It is good practice to get afloat well before the start of the race in order to check conditions, decide how to play the first beat, set the boat up for the winds found on the course, check out the favoured end of the start line, and so on. However, being on the water early and not being very active can mean that the body becomes quite cold by the time the race is due to start. This can be even more of a problem if races are postponed or there are recalls. A short 'warm-up' can help a lot!

在比赛开始前提早下水是个好习惯，这样可以检查航行条件；决定如何航行首个迎风段；根据航线上的风况调节好帆船；检查起航线上有利的一端等。不过提前下水，在水上漂着也可能意味着，越临近比赛开始身体越冷。如果比赛被推迟或有召回的情况，这可能会成为一个大问题。进行一次赛前小"热身"会有很大帮助！

Usually you would want to do this just after the orange flag gets displayed. If there are recalls or postponements, repeat if you are starting to feel cold.

通常情况下，应在橙色信号器升起后立即开始热身。如有召回或推迟，在感觉身体开始变冷时重复热身。

Here are some things you could try for one or two minutes:

花一到两分钟试试以下练习：

1. Rapid shadow boxing with a circling rather a jerking movement.
2. 快速空击练习，绕圈出拳而不是猛出拳

2. Running on the spot
2. 原地跑

3. Arm circling, forward or backward
3. 双臂前后绕圈

4. Hand and neck circling, in both directions
4. 手和脖子双向绕圈

5. Press-ups, with arms on transom or gunwale
5. 俯卧撑，双臂撑在船尾板或船舷上

Find your exercise targets by performing each of the exercises for 30 seconds and record your scores, taking a 1-minute rest between each exercise. Next session, go through the exercises in turn, doing each exercise the target number of times. Repeat the sequence three times over. Time yourself and note it down. Each time you do the circuit, try to improve your score.

为了确定练习目标，首先将每个练习做30 s，并记录次数。每个练习之间休息1 min。在下一个循环时，按照目标次数，依次完成每个练习。将这套动作重复3次。给自己计时，并记录结果。每次循环都要尝试提高次数。

You could also do a practice sail and throw in 10 tacks then bear away and do 5 gybes. This has the added advantage of getting you focused on the conditions again.

你也可以进行一次模拟驾船练习，做10次迎风转向，然后顺风偏转，做5次顺风转向。这样可以让你再次专注于当前的情形。

A Sailor's Circuit 水手循环练习

For those of you who want to go for the Olympics in ten years, and for folks who can't stand school sport, here is a 'Circuit' that you can do a number of times a week at home. It incorporates exercises for your back and hiking muscles. Make sure you warm-up and stretch before starting the circuit.

对于那些希望在十年内参加奥运会的水手，以及对学校体育运动不感兴趣的人，可以尝试以下循环练习，每周在家做几次即可。这套练习结合了背部和压舷肌肉的锻炼。确保在开始循环练习前进行热身。

1. Quadriceps: Stand on one leg with the other bent to a right angle at the knee. You can hold onto something if it helps. Bend the weight-bearing leg slowly, by about 20° only. Hold for 1 second. Then straighten the leg again. Repeat 5 times, then change legs.

股四头肌：单脚站立，另一条腿在膝盖处弯曲成直角。如有必要，可以抓住其他物品作为辅助。缓慢弯曲支撑重心（站立）的那条腿约20°即可。保持姿势1 s钟，然后伸直腿。重复5次后换腿。

CHAPTER 13 第十三章　　Physical Fitness 体　能

2. Running on the spot: Use vigorous arm movements. Lift feet about 10 cm (4 in) off the floor. Count each time the left foot touches down.
原地跑：大力摆动双臂。脚抬离地面约 10 cm（4 英寸）。计算每次左脚触地的次数。

3. Back extensor: Lie on stomach. Keeping the knees straight, lift one leg while keeping the hips in contact with the ground. Hold in the air for a moment then slowly lower. Repeat 5 times, then change legs.
背部拉伸：俯卧。保持膝盖伸直，抬起一条腿，保持髋部着地。保持姿势在空中停留片刻，然后缓慢放下。重复 5 次后换腿。

4. Sit-ups with twist: Lying on your back with fingers holding ear lobes and knees bent to 90°, sit up to touch knee with opposite elbow.
4. 转体仰卧起坐：仰卧，手指夹住耳垂，90°屈膝，坐起时，对侧肘部触膝。

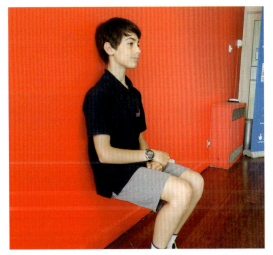

5. Wall sits: With knees and hips well bent to 90°, 'sit' with back against a wall and arms folded without sagging for 30 seconds.
5. 靠墙静蹲：双膝和臀部均弯曲 90°，双臂交叉，靠着墙"坐"（蹲）30 s，保持身体不下沉。

123

6. Back flexor / abdominal strengthening: Lie on back, knees bent 90° with feet flat on the floor and not under a bar or bench. Hands on ears, tighten abdominal muscles, keep lower back flat, slowly raise head and shoulders off the floor until in half sitting position. Then slowly lower to starting position. Breathe out on raising and breathe in on lowering.

6. 背屈肌／腹部强化：仰卧，90°屈膝，双脚平放在地板上，而不是横杆或凳子下面。双手放在耳朵上，收紧腹部肌肉，保持下背部平直，缓慢将头和肩膀抬离地面，直到半坐。然后缓慢降低回到起始位置。身体往上时呼气，下降时吸气。

8. Press-ups: Ensure you hold your body straight and your arms go down to 90°.

8. 俯卧撑：确保身体挺直，双臂下降至90°。

9. Isometric medial quadriceps: Sit with legs straight, hands placed just above kneecaps. Contract quads, particularly the part on the inside of the thigh. Count to 5, then relax.

9. 股内侧肌静力收缩：坐姿，双腿伸直，双手置于膝盖上方。收紧股四头肌，尤其是大腿内侧。数5个数，然后放松。

7. Walk around your feet: Start in press-up position and using arms only 'walk' in a circle around your feet. If you don't have room for a full circle, go from side to side through 90° and count the 'cycles'.

7. 俯身绕腿：从俯卧撑姿势开始，只用双臂绕双脚"走"一圈。如果没有空间绕一整圈，就从一边"走"到另一边，转90°，边做边数"圈数"。

CHAPTER 13 第十三章   Physical Fitness 体 能

10. Step-ups: On to a stout chair or bench. Step up with one foot, follow with the other foot, lower first foot to floor, bring the other foot down, repeat.

10. 上下台阶：准备一张结实的椅子或长凳。一只脚踏上去，另一只脚跟随，然后先踏的那只脚先下到地面，另一只脚跟着从台阶上下来，然后来回重复。

Stamina
耐力

To build up stamina you should aim to jog, run, cycle or swim for at least 20 minutes three times a week. A fanatic could try an 'Aerobic Trail':

- Jog—5 minutes
- 慢跑——5 min
- Squat thrusts—30 seconds
- 俯撑跳——30 s
- Run at half speed—2 minutes
- 半速跑——2 min
- Press-ups—30 seconds
- 俯卧撑——30 s
- Run fast 100 m, jog 100 m—2 minutes
- 快跑 100 m，慢跑 100 m——2 min
- Bent knee sit-ups—30 seconds
- 屈膝仰卧起坐——30 s
- Run at half speed—2 minutes
- 半速跑——2 min
- Run on the spot, high knee raise—30 seconds
- 原地跑，高抬膝——30 s
- Run at half speed—2 minutes
- 半速跑——2 min
- Run fast 100m, jog 100m—2 minutes
- 快跑 100 m，慢跑 100 m——2 min
- Jog—2 minutes
- 慢跑——2 min

Hiking
压舷

There was a high incidence of knee problems when most sailors hiked draped over the gunwale with knees bent and body in an 'S' shape. It has been demonstrated that hiking 'Laser style', with knees bent no more than 20°, is less likely to cause knee injury. This is because the sideways pull of the main quadriceps muscle is balanced when the knee is straight by the pull of the medial quadriceps muscle. This muscle ceases to work effectively when the knee is bent more than 20°. The result is that the kneecap slips outwards and rubs on the outer ridge of the femur, causing wear and pain.

大多数水手习惯坐在船舷上压舷，膝盖弯曲，身体呈"S"形，这样很容易导致膝盖问题的产生。应采用"激光式"压舷，双膝弯曲不超过20°，这样就能大大降低膝盖受损的可能性。这是因为，当膝盖伸直时，股直肌的侧向拉力与股内侧肌的拉力平衡。如果膝盖弯曲超过20°，股内侧肌就无法有效工作。导致膝盖骨向外滑动，摩擦股骨外脊，引发磨损和疼痛。

Try to hike like Laser sailors. Set your straps tight and high in the boat and sit out with knees bent no more than 20°. With practice this will be no more agonising than hiking in an S-shape, and you will have the benefit of being further from the water and less likely to be hit by waves. The special exercises for the medial quadriceps (circuit No.1 and No.9) are well worth doing.

试着像激光水手一样压舷。将压舷带拉紧并调高。压舷时坐到船外，双膝弯曲不超过20°。反复练习，这样操作绝对比S型压舷舒服得多，而且你离水面更远，撞浪的可能性更低。可以多做一做股内侧肌的专项训练（循环练习第1和第9项）。

Do not train with weights! While your back is growing as the ends of the bones are soft. Using weights in training can permanently damage your back, leading to back pain and weakness for the rest of your life.

不要负重训练！你的背部还处在发育中，骨骼末端较软。负重训练会对背部造成永久性损伤，导致你的后半生都承受背部疼痛和乏力。

Hiking correctly with knees bent no more than 20°
正确的压舷姿势，双膝弯曲不超过20°

Eating For Energy, Fluid For Fitness
吃出能量，喝出体能

Energy is stored in your body as something called glycogen. It is important to have as much of this as possible in your body when you arrive at a major competition.

能量以糖原的形式储存在我们的身体内。在即将参加一场重大的比赛前，应尽可能多地在身体内储存糖原。

In The Week Before The Competition:
比赛前一星期：

1. Eat plenty of complex carbohydrates—bread, cereals, spaghetti, rice, potatoes, beans, peas, lentils, root vegetables, fruit (bananas are brilliant), biscuits, cereal, muesli bars, cakes, puddings, sweet and fruit yoghurts, fruit juice. This will top your energy supply up as you near the event.
多吃复合碳水化合物——面包、麦片、意大利面、米饭、土豆、豆子、豌豆、扁豆、根茎类蔬菜、水果（香蕉就很棒）、饼干、麦片、谷物棒、蛋糕、布丁、甜酸奶和水果酸奶、果汁。在临近比赛时，这些食物能帮助你补充能量。

2. Cut down your training.
适当减少训练。

3. Avoid large meals. Eat little and often and increase your fluid intake.
避免大餐。少食多餐，增加液体摄入量。

At The Regatta 在帆船赛场

Before the regatta, find an 'energy bar' that you like and take enough to save the need for shopping. Chocolate bars contain mostly 'simple carbohydrates' and only give a short boost and should be avoided. Muesli bars are much better.

在比赛前，找到一款你喜欢的能量棒，储存足量，减少购买需要。巧克力棒主要含有"简单碳水化合物"，只能提供短暂的能量，应避免食用。谷物棒更好一些。

On the night before the regatta, have a good meal well before going to bed.

在比赛前一晚，睡觉前好好吃一顿。

On the morning of the regatta, have a high carbohydrate breakfast with plenty of fluids. Complex carbohydrates are best. Allow yourself several hours to digest food properly before racing starts. Avoid being tempted by a big fry-up which is mostly protein with little energy value.

在比赛的早上，要吃高碳水化合物早餐，摄入大量水分。复合碳水化合物最佳。在比赛开始前，给自己预留几个小时的时间好好消化食物。拒绝油炸食物的诱惑，它们主要含蛋白质，能量价值小。

If the start is late, then consider an extra pasta pot mid-morning.

如果比赛开始时间较晚，可以考虑在上午的中间再吃一杯意面。

Try to eat simply during the regatta. Choose foods you are used to, avoid shellfish and undercooked or spicy food, and drink plenty of fluids.

在比赛中应保持饮食简单。选择自己习惯的食物，避免贝类、未煮熟或辛辣的食物，多补充水分。

Make sure you eat something and drink something between every race even if you don't feel hungry or thirsty.

在每场比赛之间，务必要进食进水，即使你不觉得饥饿或口渴。

Drink 饮品

During the event, and in training, sip fluid regularly. Before competing, drink 250–500 ml of cold water; urine formation is reduced during exercise so 'pit stops' will not be necessary. At hot venues you will perspire more and will need to drink more. Avoid salt tablets—you don't need them—and isotonic high calorie drinks for sailing events, because they cause a surge of blood sugar that can increase your production of urine. Stick to water, weak squash or dilute fruit juices.

在比赛和训练期间，定期饮水。在比赛前可以饮用250~500 ml的冷水；在运动期间，尿液形成减少，因此不需要中途解决。在炎热的活动场地，你会更容易出汗，需要多喝水。避免食用盐片和航海专用的等渗高热量饮料——你并不需要这些东西，它们会使血糖激增，导致尿多。坚持饮用水、淡蔬菜汁或稀释果汁。

Eat and drink something before every race
在每场比赛前进食进水

After Races 赛后

Take fluid and some carbohydrates, preferably 'complex', starting as soon as possible after the race finishes. At the end of the day's racing, start refuelling immediately with a complex carbohydrate to give the glycogen stores as long as possible to build up. On coming ashore, the feeding process will continue.

在每轮比赛结束后，尽快补充水分和一些碳水化合物，最好是"复合碳水化合物"。在全部比赛结束后，立刻开始补充复合碳水化合物，给自己的身体足够的时间储存糖分。上岸后也要继续补充。

On The Way To The Venue
前往赛场

Often to get from home to an event involves a long car journey or maybe even a ferry or flight.

通常，从家到活动场地需要开很长时间的车，甚至可能需要乘坐轮渡或飞机。

If possible, arrive in plenty of time the night before an event so you have time to relax and recover.

如可行，在活动前一晚抵达，预留很长的时间，这样你就有时间放松和恢复。

On the journey try to keep active—play games or chat. Don't forget to eat and drink while you are travelling. Ideally prepare good healthy food before the journey. It's too easy to stop at a service station and buy unhealthy snacks!

在旅途中尽量保持活跃，可以玩游戏或聊天。不要忘记吃东西，喝水。最好在旅行前准备好各种健康的食物。要不然很容易在服务站停车的时候买一些垃圾食品。

Using your phone or watching films in the car can help make the journey pass, but it's a really good idea to switch them off half an hour before you arrive at the venue. Start chatting for the final half hour and start your mental preparation for the event—visualising it.

在车上玩手机或看电影能让旅途过得更快，但是最好在抵达场地前半小时都关掉。最后的半个小时可以聊聊天，并开始做心理准备——想象比赛的进行。

TOP TIP 重要提示

In the final half hour of your journey, go through what you are going to do at the venue: what the day's going to be like, what you will be doing about food and so on. Use this valuable time for mental rehearsal so you are ready to go once you arrive!

在抵达场地前的最后半小时，回顾一下你将要在赛场做的事情：今天是什么流程，餐饮要怎么解决等。利用好这段宝贵的时间进行心理排练，以便到达目的地后能够立即开始行动。

Seasickness
晕船

There are a number of ways you can prevent seasickness:

有多种方法可以防止晕船：

1. Take seasickness tablets. Try different kinds at home until you find one that doesn't make you feel ill. Take them in the dose and at the times described in the information sheets.

   服用晕船药。在家里尝试不同的晕船药，直到找到一种不会让感到不适的药物。按照说明书描述的剂量和时间服用。

2. Take sweets with you and suck regularly—barley sugar, peppermint, glucose.

   随身携带糖果，定期吃一点——大麦糖、薄荷糖、葡萄糖。

3. Keep busy, keep sailing, particularly if you start feeling tired which is one of the first signs of trouble. Don't just stop and bob up and down!

   保持忙碌，持续航行，尤其是当你开始感到疲倦时，这是晕船最初的征兆之一。不要停下来，要随着船上下颠簸！

4. Between races, stand up and keep your eye on the horizon rather than on the waves or the tossing boat.

   在比赛间隙，站起来看着地平线，而不是海浪或摇晃的船只。

5. Keep warm—cold people are sick quicker! Do onboard warm-up exercises.

   保暖——寒冷的人更容易晕船！在船上做一些热身运动。

6. Think positive. 'Great weather for surfing!', 'I can hack this!', 'Let's get down to work!'; not 'Yuk! I hate this. I'm going to be sick soon!'.

   进行积极思考："真是个滑浪的好天气！""这个我行的！""让我们开始航行吧！"而不是，"呸！晕船好讨厌，我快要吐了！"

7. If all else fails, you can be sick and win yacht races. Many of the best sailors feel uneasy in a confused sea, but they don't let it beat them. Chuck up and get on with the race! Keep your mind on the job and don't let it damage your efficiency and resolve to race effectively.

   如果这些方法都行不通，你依旧可以晕着船赢得比赛。许多优秀的水手在混乱的大海中都会感到不适，但不会就此被打倒。吐就吐吧，然后振作精神，继续比赛！专注航行，不要让不适影响你的效率，坚定信念高效航行。

PARENTS & COACHES
父母 & 教练

PART 6 第六部分

CHAPTER 14 第十四章
For Parents 写给父母

A Push Too Far?
给予过多压力?

We all know the popularly-held image of the Optimist parent, towering over a crying child on the slipway, shouting 'I told you to go left up the beat!'. Of course, the vast majority of Optimist parents are not like that, but the few that are give the rest a bad name. We all want our child to do well and we get excited when they succeed and downhearted when something goes wrong. The average parent at a regatta:

谈起OP水手的父母,我们的头脑中总是会浮现出一个普遍形象——他们俯视着坡道上哭泣的孩子,大声喊道:"我都跟你说过要从左侧跑迎风段!"当然,绝大多数OP水手的父母不是这样的,但少数人坏了他们的名声。我们都希望我们的孩子取得好成绩,当他们成功时我们会感到兴奋,出现问题时我们会很沮丧。在帆船赛现场的家长一般具有以下特质:

1. Is ambitious for their child's success
   对孩子的成功寄予厚望
2. Has invested heavily in gear, clothing, petrol and accommodation, and has spent many weekends doing nothing except follow the Optimist circuit
   在装备、衣物、交通和住宿上投入大量资金,在无数个周末他们什么都不做,带着孩子们到处去参加各种OP比赛
3. Can think of a list of things he or she could be doing elsewhere
   能够列出一堆他们在其他地方需要做的事情
4. Is unable to see what's happening afloat, and is cheered then depressed by garbled progress reports from those parents with high powered binoculars
   无法看到水上的情况,听到那些使用高倍双筒望远镜的父母传来的各种含糊不清的消息,时而欢呼雀跃,时而又很沮丧
5. In general, feels their child could and should do better
   一般来说,觉得他们的孩子可以而且应该做得更好

Obligation & Failure 责任 & 失败

None of the above points will help the child be a better sailor, but they can give the child feelings of obligation and failure, adding to the stress of competitive dinghy racing. The young sailor in question may be ambitious and talented, or of average ability and motivation. He or she may sail for a number of reasons that have not occurred to the parents:

以上这些行为是无法帮助孩子们成为更好的水手的,反而会增加他们的责任感和失败感,使本来就竞争激烈的帆船比赛变得压力更大。年少的水手们或者雄心勃勃、才华横溢,或者资质平平、动机不强——他们航海的原因可能完全出乎父母的意料:

- Independence afloat
- 在水上独立航行
- Because friends sail
- 因为自己的朋友航海
- Good fun messing about in boats
- 玩船很快乐
- Been pushed into it by parents, but would much rather 'Listen to music, get onto my computer, go riding, play mini Rugby'
- 被父母逼迫,更愿意自己"听听音乐、玩电脑、骑马、玩迷你橄榄球"

Good Optimist Parent 优秀的 OP 父母	Bad Optimist Parent 糟糕的 OP 父母
Wants their child to enjoy sailing 希望他们的孩子享受帆船运动	Wants their child to win at all costs 不惜一切想要孩子赢
Lets their child learn & make mistakes 鼓励学习 & 允许犯错	Over controls their child 过度控制孩子
Lets their child have fun 让孩子玩得开心	Creates a pressurised atmosphere 给孩子制造压力
Lets their child make decisions 让孩子自己做决定	Tells their child what to do 告诉他们要做什么
Praises their child 表扬他们	Criticises their child 批评孩子
Respects & supports the coach 尊重并支持教练	Criticises & argues with the coach 批评教练，和教练争吵

The Reasons Why 为什么会这样

As parents we must look at why we take our children sailing. Is it frustrated ambition on our part, or because we feel we have something worthwhile to pass on to the child? We can seek to inspire our children with our enthusiasm and delight in sailing but have to allow them to find it for themselves. They are at an impressionable age and will certainly do what we want them to do, but the time will come when they will lose interest in the sport if they are not finding their own reasons to continue with it.

作为父母，我们必须想清楚为什么要让孩子学习航海。是因为我们自己未能实现的抱负，还是想要将一些有价值的东西传递给孩子？我们可以用我们对航海的热情和喜爱来激励孩子们，但必须让他们自己去探索。他们正处于易受影响的年龄，肯定会按照我们的想法去做。但是如果没有找到自己继续这项运动的理由，他们迟早会失去兴趣。

We must be sensitive to our children's attitude to competition, and to their aims in sailing and their everyday lives. Very few people are able to win national and international championships or the Olympics. We must support our children at the standard they wish to compete at, rather than constantly implying that they should be doing better than they are.

我们必须对孩子们的竞争态度，以及他们在航海和日常生活中的目标保持敏感。能够赢得全国和国际冠军或奥运会奖牌的人是少数。我们必须支持孩子们，但要按照他们的竞争标准，而不是一直暗示他们应该做得比现在更好。

Parental Support
父母的支持

There are a few key elements of support that we can provide our children:

我们可以为孩子们提供的一些关键支持：

- Physical: Home, security, accommodation
- 物质上：家庭、安全感、住处
- Emotional: Understanding, insight, comforting, supportive, loving father / mother figures, dependable, predictable, consistent, realistic, and inspirational
- 情感上：理解、洞察力、安慰、支持、慈爱的父亲 / 母亲形象、可靠、可预测、始终如一、理解现实且鼓舞人心
- Financial: Funding for boats, equipment, clothing, travel, accommodation, entry fees
- 经济上：提供船只、装备、衣物、旅行、住宿、报名等事项的费用
- Logistical: Transport to home club for training, open meetings, national and international events, arranging accommodation, feeding

afloat and ashore
- 后勤：负责接送孩子们去俱乐部参加培训、公开赛、全国和国际赛事，安排住宿、水上岸上的餐饮
- Bosun: Checking, repair, maintenance, launching and landing assistance
- 船务员：船只检查、维修、维护、上下水协助
- Facilitator: All the time
- 协调者：自始至终

Parents can help and support without taking over
父母可以在不干涉孩子的前提下提供帮助和支持

A Bad Result 面对糟糕的比赛成绩

Don't start listing what went wrong as soon as they come ashore. Let them do the talking if they want to; if they don't, try to avoid discussion of events until emotions have cooled. Try to work out your child's recovery time. After a bad race, competitors of all ages need a time to recover emotionally, before being able to think clearly and analytically.

不要孩子们一上岸就立即让他们列举出了什么问题。如果他们想要聊聊的话，就让他们说；如果他们不想，就尽量避免谈论比赛的事情，直到他们的情绪平复下来。试着了解孩子赛后恢复所需的时间。在一场糟糕的比赛后，任何年龄的参赛者都有一个情绪恢复期，然后才能清晰地思考和分析。

Give some thought to your reaction to seeing them sail the worst race of their life. How long do you need to recover before you can:

想一想你在看到了他们一生中最糟糕的一场比赛后，需要多长时间恢复，才能：
- Be civil to anybody?
- 对他人礼貌？
- Bring yourself to look at the child?
- 去看看孩子的状态？
- Speak to the child?
- 和孩子说话？
- Control your body language (hunched shoulders, glowering face, irritable movements)?
- 控制你的肢体语言（耸肩、满脸怒气、动作焦躁）？
- Discuss the race objectively, without your disappointment being transferred to the child?
- 客观地讨论比赛，而不是将你的失望转移到孩子身上？

The Child's View 孩子的视角

Your child may well know more about sailing than you will ever do and will certainly know more about what happened afloat. They may be bitterly disappointed by their result, know that you will be disappointed, and will feel wretched before you utter a word. In such circumstances some young sailors do not want to come ashore to face their parents' reaction.

孩子很可能比你更了解帆船运动，而且他们肯定更清楚水上发生的事情。他们可能会对自己的成绩感到非常失望，知道你也很失望，在你说任何话之前，他们就已经感到很难受了。在这种情况下，有些年少的水手甚至都不想上岸去面对父母的反应。

Try not to say a word; give them a squeeze and put their boat away. Later that night, after relaxing and eating, you will both be in a better frame of mind to take a logical and realistic look at the situation. Show them that whatever happens you love them and think they are great!

试着什么都不要说；给他们一个紧紧的拥抱，帮他们把船收起来。在当天晚些时候，放松和吃完饭以后，你们双方的心情都会更好一些，能够理性现实地看待问题。让他们知道无

Treat them in the same way whether they win or lose and try to act naturally on the drive home even after a total disaster. Do be sensitive to their needs, and considerate of their moods. Give your child space to develop as an independent person. Try to work out what your child really feels about competing—is it just to please you? Praise and emphasise the good things your child did in the racing. Build up their self-esteem and beware the careless comment that may put them down.

无论输赢，都要以同样的方式对待他们，即使当天的比赛糟糕透了，也要尝试在开车回家的路上表现得很自然。敏锐地体察他们的需求，体谅他们的情绪。给予孩子们独立发展的空间。试着弄清楚孩子对竞争的真实感受——只是为了让你高兴吗？表扬并强调他们比赛中做得好的方面。建立他们的自尊，注意自己的言论，不要随口说一些贬低他们的评论使他们失望。

- Do have realistic aspirations for your child
- 对孩子们的期望切合实际
- Don't use sarcasm at any time
- 任何时候都不要讽刺他们
- Do encourage your children to take part in other sports
- 鼓励孩子们参加其他运动
- Don't fall out openly with other parents, or upset your child's opponents
- 不要公开与其他父母争吵或惹恼孩子的对手
- Let the coach do the coaching; do not undermine him or her
- 让教练做自己的工作；不要毁坏他们的权威

Parents With Coaching Ability
具备教学能力的父母

Be careful not to limit your child's ability to use his own knowledge and judgement. The sailor must be encouraged to develop the ability to coach themselves, to analyse their performance objectivity, and plan the aims of their own training. They must decide their own tactics after listening to the opinions of 'expert'.

注意不要限制孩子运用自身所学和自己的判断能力。一定要鼓励孩子发展自学能力，客观地分析自己的表现，为自己制定培训目标。在听取"专家"的意见后，必须自行决定自己的策略。

Knowledgeable parents should seek to work with the coach. If they do not agree with aspects of their teaching or sailor-handling, they should talk the matter over quietly in private.

知识渊博的父母应该寻求与教练的合作。如果他们不同意教练的教学或对待学员的方式，应该私底下平心静气地和教练讨论。

A coach who is also a parent must not favour their own child and must ensure that their child relates to them only as a coach in the sailing environment when they are working. Otherwise the coach will lose objectivity.

同时，如果孩子的父母即为孩子的教练，不得偏袒他们。并且必须确保在工作时，孩子只将他们视作教练。否则他们就无法客观地进行教学。

International Championships
国际锦标赛

Parents are a valuable and necessary part of an international sailing team. The coach will, of course, take responsibility for training and racing matters but, as at home, the competitors will benefit from the support of one or more of their parents who can fill the following functions:

家长是国际帆船队中宝贵且必要的组成部分。当然，训练和比赛事宜由教练来负责，但是就像在家一样，参赛者会受益于一个或多个父母的支持，父母们可以履行以下职能：

Manager / team leader: Responsible for air flights, accommodation, communication with the organisation, going to meetings, living with the team and looking after their needs such as food, laundry, health care, transport and off the water activities.

经理/团队负责人：负责航班、住宿、团队沟通、参加会议、与团队一起生活并照顾他的需求，如准备食物、洗衣物、健康护理、辅助交通和水上活动。

Bosun: Transporting and packing boats, checking and setting up charter boats to suit each sailor, modification of boats during measurement, on-going repairs, help afloat during training, launching and recovery assistance, security.

船务员： 负责运输和打包船只；检查并调试租用的帆船，使其适应他们的孩子；在船只丈量时，修改船只；持续维修；协助水上训练；协助上下水；安全保障。

Helping The Coach 协助教练

Most parents will, of course, come as spectators, but almost invariably their children will appreciate their presence even if they do not acknowledge it. It's always good having supporters about, and the team will be lifted by them. If there is a serious problem with a child, their parent's unique experience can also be invaluable in sorting matters out.

当然，大多数父母的身份是旁观者，即使孩子们不会明说，但他们总是会希望自己的父母在场。有人支持总是好的，而且家长团队会使孩子们备受鼓舞。如果有的孩子出现严重问题，自己父母的独特经验对解决问题会起到十分宝贵的作用。

A parent may be asked by the coach or team leader to keep an eye on the noticeboard for changes to the sailing instructions, collection of results, notices of protests against competitors, notices of meetings, and so on. Parents can also be very useful in helping to get boats measured, being careful to minimise the effects of this stressful time on the competitors.

教练或领队可能会安排一些家长留意公告栏，以了解航行细则的变更、比赛成绩、竞争对手的抗议通知、会议通知等。父母在船只丈量时也会是很大助力，但要注意在这一紧张时期，应将对选手的影响降至最低。

Parents must, however, defer to the wishes of the coach if he considers that a sailor would benefit from less parental contact. It is sometimes difficult for a parent to appreciate that, in the highly charged atmosphere of an international event, their tensions are being passed on to their child.

但是，如果教练认为，在比赛期间，和父母的接触少些，水手会受益更多，那么父母应遵从教练的意愿。父母有时很难意识到，在国际赛事高度紧张的氛围中，他们的紧张情绪会传递给孩子们。

Parents can be a great support at international events
在国际赛事中，父母能提供很大的支持

CHAPTER 15 第十五章
The Perfect Coach 完美教练

Optimist coaching is a rewarding experience, from the sheer fun of a group of kids surfing and shouting their way downwind in a force 6 to the agony and pure thrill of supporting talented competitors in an international regatta.

对于一名教练来说，教授 OP 帆船的经验是非常有意义的。从看着一群孩子在六级风中大喊大叫、顺风滑浪、感受他们单纯的快乐，到支持一群才华横溢的选手在国际帆船赛上竞争，经历他们的痛苦和惊喜。

Coaching to national standard involves repeatedly going over theory until it is absorbed. Boat handling and basic exercises must be practised until boat control is reflex control, and confidence and ability are high. Top national sailors will mostly have the knowledge to get to top international standard. Their challenge is to use that knowledge effectively. This requires a different kind of coaching in which encouragement, facilitation, and technical support become more important, as the competitor develops his own sailing and self-coaching skills.

按照国家级水平的标准进行教学，需要一遍又一遍地复习理论，直到学员完全吸收。控船操作和基础练习必须持续进行，直到学员对船只的控制形成条件反射，并且具备很强的自信和能力。顶尖的国家水手所具备的理论知识大多达到最高国际级别。他们面临的挑战是，如何有效地运用这些知识。这需要教练采用一种不同的教学方式，对学员的鼓励、促进以及技术上的支持会更加重要，因为参赛者一般能够发展自己的航海水平，且具备自我教学的技能。

The step between top national and top international standard is enormous. Sailors fail to grasp the amount of work required. The coach is teacher / trainer, friend, performance analyst, motivator, disciplinarian, counsellor, facilitator, technical expert, researcher, manager / administrator and publicity agent.

国家顶级水手和国际顶级水手之间存在巨大的差距，水手们一般难以理解其中的工作量。教练需要扮演各种角色，他们是老师 / 培训师、朋友、表现分析师、激励者、约束者、顾问、协调者、技术专家、研究员、管理者 / 行政人员和宣传代理人。

Teaching 教学

Teaching advanced racing knowledge and skills is a prime function of an Optimist coach.

一名 OP 教练的主要职责是，教授高级竞赛知识和技术。

Training 培训

This involves setting up appropriate exercises afloat and ashore to aid development of top racing skills.

培训包括设置合理的水上水下的练习，以帮助水手们发展顶尖竞赛技能。

Planning 计划

The racing year must be planned around major targeted events to enable the racers to reach peak performance at those times. Every year's training programme should cover all aspects of dinghy racing. With national team selection trials in April / May and major national and international championships in July / August, squads in the northern hemisphere should run through the winter, with polishing sessions before the championships.

帆船竞赛年度计划必须围绕重大目标赛事进行安排，以使选手能够在这些比赛中达到巅峰状态。每年的训练计划应涵盖小帆船比赛的各个方面。由于国家队选拔赛在4月或5月开展，重要的国家和国际锦标赛则是在7月或8月，位于北半球的帆船训练队应组织在冬季集训，并在锦标赛前进行技术打磨训练。

Talks & Discussions 理论讲解 & 讨论

A young person's attention span varies from about 5 minutes at age ten to 20 minutes plus at age fifteen. Plan to break talks with questions, demonstrations, pictures or a quiz to maintain interest. Talks must be short and simple, but not childish. Complex concepts must be explained clearly and simply using drawings, model boats and demonstration. Lengthy boring topics like the racing rules can be covered in 10-minute blocks, with revision during debriefs when actual incidents are discussed. Be prepared to abort a talk and go afloat if the audience's concentration is lost.

年轻人的专注时长会随着年龄的增长有所不同，在10岁时大约5 min，到15岁时则大约20 min。教练应做好计划，将问题、演示、图片或小测试等环节穿插在教学中，以保持学员的兴趣。讲解必须简短明了，不要过于幼稚。复杂概念的解释必须简单清晰，可采用画画、船模和演示的方式进行讲解。像竞赛规则这样冗长乏味的话题可以在10 min内讲完，在最后总结、讨论实际事件时进行复习。如果学员注意力不集中，随时准备停下讲解，直接下水。

Use 'Speak Show Do': describe something, demonstrate it, and then get them to try it. In their first year, younger sailors may not retain or fully appreciate the significance of some information but, after going over the subject for a couple of years, the same sailors become capable of giving the lectures!

使用"说－演示－做"的方法：先用语言进行描述，然后演示，之后再让学员们尝试去做。在学习航海的第一年，年轻的水手们可能无法记住或完全理解某些信息的重要性，但是在重复同样的主题几年之后，同一批水手甚至会具备授课的能力！

Use regular recall to fix things in the mind. This can be done before starting on the main topic of the day or can be brought into the 'debrief' periods.

定期回顾，巩固记忆。回顾工作可在开始当天的主要内容之前完成，也可以在总结阶段进行。

It is very effective when top sailors comment and contribute as much as possible. Plan talks when sailors are fresh—first thing, or after lunch. Advanced topics can be covered at the end of the day as an option for more mature competitors.

尽可能地让顶尖的水手积极参与、发表评论，这会使培训非常高效。应计划在学员清醒的时候进行理论讲解——活动一开始或午餐之后。对于更成熟的选手来说，一些高级课题可在一天训练结束时选择性开展。

A coaching session
在培训课上

Communication 沟通

Do your very best to prevent any sailor losing face during training. Don't use sarcasm, make jokes or encourage laughter at the expense of young or sensitive individuals.

尽全力避免在培训期间让任何水手丢面子。不要消费年轻或敏感的学员，讽刺他们，开玩笑或者鼓励相互的嘲笑。

Don't use questions that imply that a sailor has or may have made an error. It is better to avoid starting questions with 'Why?' as this implies criticism. Try starting with 'What? When? Where? How much? How many?'. Help competitors to express how they are getting on and what they think about something, by developing an effective questioning technique.

不要用提问的方式暗示学员犯了错或者可能犯了错。最好避免以"为什么？"开头，因为这存在批评暗示。尝试以"什么？什么时候？哪里？多少？"这样的疑问词开头提出问题，发展有效提问的技巧，帮助选手们说明自己的进展以及对事情的看法。

Start with general questions and then focus down to more specific questions using simple words. If you ask a question you must listen carefully to the answer, think about it, and use their words to shape the next question. This will increase a sailor's awareness and will help them formulate new answers and ideas. Above all, keep the fun in all aspects of training and competition, with varied activities and lots of breaks for snacks.

开始时，先询问学员一般性的问题，然后使用简单的语言聚焦更具体的问题。如果你问了他们一个问题，就必须要仔细地倾听答案，并进行思考，然后用他们的语言来提下一个问题。这会提高水手的意识，帮助他们形成新的答案和想法。除此以外，还要组织各种丰富的活动，并给学员们大量的时间休息和吃零食，从而保持在训练和比赛各方面的乐趣。

Typical Training Day Timetable
典型的单日培训时间表

09:00	Get changed, rigged and ready to sail 换衣服，装船，准备下水
10:00	Recall of practical and theoretical points from previous day 回顾前一天的实操和理论知识
10:05	Talk / discussion 理论讲解 / 讨论
10:25	Racing rules (one rule or incident) 竞赛规则（一条规则或一个比赛事件）
10:35	Briefing and goal setting for the day 简述并设定当日培训目标
10:40	Launch 下水
10:55	Boat handling 控船练习
11:25	Starting exercises 起航练习
13:00	Ashore 回岸
13:15	Debrief / video / lunch 总结 / 视频 / 午餐
13:30	Talk / discussion / rules 理论讲解 / 讨论 / 规则
13:50	Briefing 简述
13:55	Launch 下水
14:10	Boatspeed work (in pairs) 船速练习（两人一组）
14:30	Match racing 对抗赛
15:45	Race (long) 比赛（长时间）
17:00	Ashore, change, boats away 回岸，换衣服，收船
17:20	Debrief / video / tea 总结 / 视频 / 茶点
17:40	Chats with individual sailors 水手单人沟通
18:00	Home 回家

Briefing / Debriefing 简述 / 总结

Before going afloat, it is important to outline the aim of the session, and to detail the activities that will take place.

在下水之前，务必概述训练目的，并详细说明将要进行的活动，这一点很重要。

On returning ashore, each activity will be discussed, and their values assessed. Each sailor should be encouraged to say how they got on. Any incidents can be talked through, and lessons drawn. The debrief is probably the most important session of the day, for here fun afloat can be used to illustrate important points of theory in an easily understood way. At the end of any session it is vital that the sailors are able to have a chat with you privately to air a problem or to sort out an idea.

回岸后，讨论每项练习并评估其培训价值。鼓励每个水手说一说自己的状态如何。可以讨论任何事件，并从中吸取教训。总结也许是一天训练中最重要的环节，因为在这个时候，通过讨论有趣的水上活动可以很容易就说明重要的理论观点。在训练结束后，水手们与教练的私下沟通十分重要，有益于他们提出问题或梳理自己的想法。

Getting To Know The Sailors
了解水手们

- Spend a lot of time together in training, and learn how they react afloat and ashore, body language used, and so on.
- 长期与学员一起训练，了解他们在水上和岸上的反应，使用的肢体语言等。
- Always be available for a chat about anything at the sailing club, at home, and on the phone.
- 让他们随时可以和你沟通任何事情，无论是在帆船俱乐部还是家里，或是打电话。
- Get to know each sailor's parents, home situation and ability at school, in order to be aware of outside influences.
- 了解每个水手的父母、家庭情况和在校表现，以便知晓他们所受的外部影响。
- Recognise an individual's response to the stress of competition and help each person to find ways of coping.
- 理解个人面对竞争压力时的反应，并帮助每个人找到应对方法。
- Recognise how best to give support when things go wrong. Emotions can be difficult — anger, frustration or disappointment must be controlled or contained, or performance will suffer.
- 知道在出现问题时，如何给予最好的支持。处理情绪可能会很难——愤怒、沮丧或失望必须得到控制或抑制，否则他们的表现就会受到影响。
- Get to know a sailor's social skills—the ability to fit in a group and interact happily. Shy loners need help to establish their place in the group.
- 了解水手的社交技能——融入团队并愉快互动的能力。有些人比较害羞，不喜交际，需要他人的帮助来建立在群体中的位置。

Performance Analysis
表现分析

Performance analysis should be done in a number of different ways:

应采用几种不同的方式进行表现分析：

- By the coach: Use careful observation to identify strengths and weaknesses.
- 通过教练：仔细观察，识别学员的优劣势。
- By the sailor: Use post-race questionnaires and target charts. The coach may spot unrecognised weaknesses.
- 通过水手自己：使用赛后问卷和目标图表。教练可能会发现未被察觉的弱点。
- By another sailor: Use a pair-training buddy.
- 通过另一名水手：由同组（两人一组）的训练伙伴评析。

Watch for competitors who set themselves unrealistic goals and are never satisfied as a result. Encourage realistic goal setting.

注意选手们为自己设定的目标，如果非常不切实际，他们会因无法达成目标而永不满足。鼓励选手们为自己制定可实现的目标。

CHAPTER 15 第十五章　The Perfect Coach 完美教练

Building Confidence 树立自信

Encourage logs or scrapbooks—with each good result confidence will grow. Some sailors, particularly girls, find starting difficult due to pushy, over-confident children. Tell them they're good, remind them of successes, do exercises in which they have to get to certain points on the line under pressure. Make sure they know the starting rules backwards and can shout 'Protest' and keep concentrating on the start all at the same time. Promote confidence in being able to sail in any weather, anytime, anywhere, so they know that there is nothing to fear from wind and water.

鼓励学员写日志或制作剪贴簿——每次取得好成绩都会增强他们的信心。有些水手，尤其是女孩会觉得起航非常困难，因为总是会在起航线上碰到一些咄咄逼人、过于自信的孩子。告诉他们，其实他们很棒，提醒他们曾经取得的成功。可以做一些练习，让他们在压力下到达起航线的特定位置。确保他们对起航规则了如指掌，可以做到在大喊"抗议"的同时专注于起航。增强他们在任何天气、任何时间、任何地点航行的信心，让他们知道风和水没有什么可怕的。

Giving Praise 表扬

Look for things to praise in all sailors but be selective with praise in top performers—praise effort and performance more than results.

寻找所有水手身上值得称赞的优点，但要有选择性地表扬那些顶尖的水手——多多赞美他们的付出和表现，而不仅仅是比赛结果。

Believe in his / her potential, but do not expect faultless, perfect and mature sailing all the time. When an error occurs, don't hold back praise for the good sailing. Remember that sailors do not mean to make errors; they will recognise them and will feel deeply disappointed with a poor result.

相信他／她的潜力，但不要期望他们能够一直保持毫无瑕疵、成熟完美的航行状态。在出错时，也不要吝惜赞美曾经表现优异的时候。请记住，水手们并不是故意犯错的；他们会意识到自己的错误并对糟糕的成绩感到非常失望。

We have all been in the situation where we have known exactly what to do, but in the race everything went wrong. It is one of the marvellous things about sailing that conditions vary constantly, and victory is seldom certain. The place of the coach is to support rather than criticise.

我们都曾经历过这样的情况：我们完全知道该怎么做，但在比赛中一切都不顺利。航海的奇妙之处就在于，条件不断变化，胜利几乎没有绝对。教练的职责是支持学员而不是批评他们。

As well as formal sessions, go through things in the boat park
像平常训练一样，在停船区进行讲解

Promoting Self-Coaching 提倡自学

Encourage the sailors:
鼓励水手们：

- To think independently and objectively
- 独立客观地思考

OPTIMIST RACING OP级帆船竞赛

- To analyse their own strengths and weaknesses, and to use that knowledge to establish realistic training and long term aims
- 分析自己的优劣势，运用这些信息为自己设置切实可行的训练和长期目标
- To develop on-going performance analysis skills to enable them to monitor progress towards those aims
- 培养持续分析表现的能力，以便监督自己实现目标的进展
- To identify negative emotions and cope with them in competition
- 明确自己的不良情绪，并能在比赛中很好地处理

Team Spirit 团队精神

Optimist sailing is an individual sport but needs other sailors to help you along the way. It's very difficult to improve sailing on your own. So, even if it is an individual sport, you need to foster a team environment. This makes it more fun for everyone and the journey is more rewarding with others!

虽然OP航海是一项个人运动，但是你的成长需要其他水手的帮助。单靠自己提高航行水平是非常困难的。所以，尽管这是一项单人运动，你也需要培养良好的团队氛围。这样可以让每个人的航行都更有乐趣，而且和他人一起航海更有意义啊！

- Try logos on clothing
- 尝试将团队的logo贴在衣服上
- Try a flag or logo on boats, sailing kit, bags, cars
- 试着将旗子或logo贴在帆船上、航海装备上、包包或车上
- Use a team coach boat which easily recognisable
- 使用一艘容易辨认的团队教练艇
- Have a WhatsApp or Facebook group to improve communication
- 创建WhatsApp或脸书讨论小组，改善团队沟通
- Work on your personal image too
- 当然也努力树立你的个人形象

Team kit
团队统一装备

Discipline
纪律

Practise the behaviour you expect from your sailors; be fair, considerate, and understanding. As a coach you have to be judge and executioner, and after a long day's training you may be tired and not as discerning as usual. Certain activities, the worst of which is team racing, cause emotionally charged incidents to occur between tired sailors. Summary rulings can lead to frustration and anger, whether or not the ruling was correct.

践行你期望水手具备的行为：公平、体贴和理解。作为一名教练，你必须充当裁判和决断者。虽然经过一天漫长的训练，你可能已经很疲倦，不像平常一样敏锐。有些活动，尤其是团体赛，会导致疲惫的水手们情绪激动，从而发生冲突。快刀斩乱麻似的裁决可能会引发学员的沮丧和愤怒，无论裁决是否正确。

Minor transgressions are usually best overlooked. More serious cases may be called over to the coach boat. Usually a quiet, understanding but stern word will settle matters. If there is an argument between two squad members, call both over to the boat and sort matters out. Speak quietly and be totally fair and impartial. If it's clear that the sailor cannot control himself, suggest that he sits out the next exercise. The ultimate sanction would be to send someone ashore, but this is a rare last resort.

对于一般轻微的冲突行为，最好忽略。情况严重的，可能就需要把学员叫到教练艇上。通常，和他们进行一次平静、充满理解但严肃的沟通就能解决问题。如果两队的成员发生争执，应把双方都叫到船上进行处理。安静平和地沟通，确保公平公正。如果有的水手明显无法控制自己，就建议他不要参与下一个练习。终极处罚是让他们回岸，但这是最后的手段，并不常用。

Remember that emotional outbursts may be due not just to immediate circumstances, but also to hormonal changes of puberty, shyness, parent problems, relationship problems, money worries, or school worries.

记住，学员情绪爆发可能不仅是出于当下的情况，还可能是青春期、性格腼腆、父母问题、人际关系问题、经济担忧或学校压力，使学员的荷尔蒙产生变化。

Other Coach Roles
教练的其他角色

When at a regatta, the coach has added responsibilities:

在帆船赛中，教练的责任会增加：

- To help the sailors understand the sailing instructions, cope with protests, deal with aggravations
- 帮助水手们理解航行规则，应对抗议，处理各种烦恼
- To be an information gatherer for the team on tides, weather forecasts, expert opinion, new ideas
- 帮助团队收集有关潮汐信息、天气预报、专家意见和新的想法
- To provide or find the answer to any relevant questions, providing the information top sailors need to consider in their challenge for top results
- 提供或找到每个相关问题的答案，为顶级水手提供在竞争中所需的信息，以获得最佳成绩
- To encourage sailors to be independent decision makers on the water and responsible on the shore
- 鼓励水手们在水上独立做决策，并负责岸上的活动

Coaching Scenarios
教学场景

Being a coach isn't always the same, there are different scenarios you may be working in:

教练的工作并不是千篇一律的，你可能会经历很多不同的工作场景：

- Squad coaching of a top national, area or club group of competent racing sailors over several years. Ideal group size: 8–12.
- 几年来长期指导一个有实力的顶级国家、地区或俱乐部帆船队。理想的团队规模：8~12人。
- Short term coaching of a team in preparation for a major event.
- 为备战重大赛事的团队提供短期指导。
- Individual coaching of an outstanding top sailor. Most Olympic sailors are coached individually or share a coach with up to two other competitors. This is unusual in the Optimist class, although some parents try to fulfil this role.
- 1对1指导一名杰出的顶级水手。大多数奥运水手都是单独接受培训的，或者最多和两名其他参赛者共用一个教练。这对于OP级别并不常见，不过有些家长会尝试做这项工作。

Squad Coaching 指导训练队

With groups of 12 sailors or less, this is the most satisfying and productive arrangement. It is unusual for a sailor to be at the top of the Optimist class for more than four years. Long term coaching over this period will be very beneficial.

一个训练队人数小于等于12人最为理想且最有成效。在OP级别中，能够处于顶尖地位超过4年的水手并不常见。在此期间接受长期指导会非常有益。

A good coach will encourage his racers to listen to other experts and collect information from every possible source. Such coaching is best done on a club or area basis. Sailors should be invited to join the training group, when they are capable of completing a club race, they want to race, they are capable of self-rescue and they have suitable equipment.

一名优秀的教练会鼓励自己的学员听取其他专家的意见,并从各种可能的渠道收集信息。在俱乐部或区域比赛中,这种教学是最有成效的。教练应在选手满足适当条件时,邀请他们加入训练队——有能力完成俱乐部比赛,想要参加比赛,有能力自救并且配有合适的装备。

This type of group should ideally train for a period of at least six months.

在理想情况下,这样的训练队应该至少训练6个月。

Short Term Coaching 短期指导

Short term coaching of a team preparing for a major event usually takes the form of 2–4 weekends and a week spent at the championship venue immediately before the event. It is likely that you will know the sailors fairly well, but the training periods should be used to get to know much more about them, their attitudes to the competition, their parents and their peers.

为备战重大赛事的团队提供短期指导,通常持续2~4个周末,以及比赛前一周在实际的锦标赛场地进行训练。你可能已经比较了解水手们了,但应利用培训时间更多地了解他们,包括他们对比赛的态度、他们的父母和同伴等。

Work with each sailor, identifying their aims, and their perceived strengths and weaknesses. Develop personal plans for the training period and re-assess by phone or email mid-week after each training session. Build up an idea of how they react to stress, successes and failures. Develop a support plan for each sailor.

与大家一起训练,明确他们的目标,以及他们对自己优劣势的认知。制定培训期间的个人计划,并在每次培训课后的周中,通过电话或电子邮件重新评估。了解他们如何应对压力、成功和失败。为每个水手都制定一个支持计划。

Afloat, use buddy training for tuning, speed and windshift spotting practice; sailing up opposite sides of the course to confirm wind bends and sea breeze effects. Work on starting (particularly port end), acceleration, mid-line judging and mark rounding. Match racing develops boatspeed and race winning skills. Team racing is fun and should be used for relaxation, but it can become excessively aggressive and should be tightly controlled.

在水上训练时,两人一组,练习调船、加速和找风;两人从航线的两侧迎风航行,确认风的弯曲和海风的影响。重点训练起航(尤其是左侧起航)、加速、中间位置起航线判断和绕标。对抗赛能帮助学员提高船速和获胜技巧。团体赛充满乐趣,应用来帮助学员们放松,但也可能会使大家的攻击性变得很强,应注意严格控制。

Generally, make sure that whatever you organise allows individuals to cover their own training aims, and don't neglect to gather tidal and meteorological information for the area where the racing will be held well before the event.

总的来说,无论组织什么活动,都要确保每个学员都能够实现自己的训练目标。注意不要忘了在赛前收集比赛区域的潮汐和气象信息。

Coaching At Competitions
赛场教学

Boat Measurement 船只丈量

This is a stressful time, even if nothing is found to be wrong.

船只丈量总是让人倍感压力,即使没有发现任何问题。

You must be present to talk with the measurers about any perceived infringement. Check with an up-to-date copy of the class rules to make sure that the interpretation is correct, or that alternative interpretations may be as valid. An appeal to the chief measurer should always be considered if necessary.

CHAPTER 15 第十五章 | The Perfect Coach 完美教练

教练必须在现场与丈量人员讨论任何可能存在的违规行为。检查级别规则的最新要求，确保解读正确，或者其他解读可能也有效。如有必要，随时考虑向首席丈量员上诉。

It is good for morale to get measured as early as possible, but there is always the risk that you will get involved in that year's controversial rule interpretation. These are always sorted out before the event but can worry competitors for days. Keep cool, positive, and confident in your handling of measurement problems, and your sailors will stay calm too.

尽早检验自己的士气也是好事，但总是有风险的，你可能会卷入当年有争议的规则。虽然这些问题总是能在活动前解决，但可能会让参赛选手担心好几天。在处理丈量问题时，教练应保持冷静、积极和自信，学员也会随之保持冷静。

If modifications are needed to the boats or their gear, delegate this, if possible, to a competent parent. You must keep on top of other measurement questions, keeping the team occupied and supporting the anxious helm.

如需对船只或装备进行修改，应尽可能将其委托给有能力的家长。你必须对其他的丈量问题了如指掌，让团队保持忙碌并支持焦虑的学员。

Boat measurement can be a stressful time
让人倍感压力的船只丈量

Focus On The Competition 专注比赛

Go over the sailing instructions with the sailors as soon as they are available, and make sure they fully understand them. Recall important and unusual points at subsequent briefings.

一旦航行细则发布，应尽快与水手一起学习，并确保他们完全理解。在随后的简述中复习重要的和不常见的规则。

On the morning of the first race, keep the team focused and positive with early boat checks and rigging; plus a briefing / discussion covering tide predictions, wind, possibility of shifts, as well as the programme and arrangements for the day. The sailors must be given information clearly and accurately before going afloat.

在第一轮比赛的早上，组织团队尽早检查船只和索具，进行简述/讨论与预测潮汐、风况和风摆相关的问题以及当天的计划和安排，保持团队的专注和积极。在下水前，必须向水手提供准确清晰的信息。

Give your advice, but do not order your team to all 'Start at the port end and sail up the left side of the course'. The predictions of even top international coaches should not be trusted by sailors to the extent that they follow the plan whatever happens. A top sailor is in a better position to see what's going on in a race and should be encouraged to think for themselves and decide what to do without fear of criticism when they come ashore.

给出你的建议，但是不要命令全队人员都"从起航线左侧起航，沿着航线的左侧航行"。即使是顶级国际教练的预测，水手们也不应该全听全信。无论发生什么，都完全按计划执行。顶尖的水手能更好地看清比赛中的情况，应鼓励他们独立思考并做决定，完全不用担心上岸时会受到批评。

Afloat 水上

Use the coach boat to get out to the race area an hour before racing starts if possible, towing the team if the wind is light. Check wind and tide at both the start and windward mark area if possible, and report back to the squad by which

143

time they will have done their tuning and shift tracking runs.

如可行,在比赛开始前一小时使用教练艇前往比赛区域。如果风小,就将整个团队拖过去。可行的话,检查起航线和上风标区域的风和潮汐情况,并告知团队。那时,他们应该已经调完船,并且已进行多次风摆检测航行了。

Take a look at all sails and help readjust rigs or reassure the racers. Anchor and discuss tactics and ideas. Withdraw outside the race area when required by the sailing instructions, and watch the start if possible from the favoured end of the line.

检查所有船帆,帮助学员重新调整或鼓励安抚他们。将教练艇抛锚,和选手们讨论策略和想法。根据航行细则的要求,适时撤出比赛区域,如可行,从起航线的有利端观看起航。

The coach helping their sailors before the race
教练在赛前指点水手们

It is almost impossible to see what is going on in big fleet racing, so during the races try to relax and keep tracking wind and tide. After the race, the guys who have done well will come alongside first. Congratulate them and find out what happened, where they started, what the wind did and how their speed was.

在大型的群发赛上,几乎不可能看到发生了什么。所以在比赛期间,可以试着放轻松,持续关注风和潮汐情况。在比赛结束后,表现出色的选手会先靠过来。向他们表示祝贺,了解具体情况——他们从哪里起航的,风况怎么样以及他们的船速如何。

If you have a large group, make sure the later finishers can come alongside and talk to you. They may or may not want to talk things over. You should know them well enough to know what to do. Feed them, fix anything, and offer them the chance to come aboard for a rest. In good time for the next start, get them doing warming up exercises before focusing on the next start.

如果你指导的团队较大,应确保最后完成比赛的选手能来到你旁边和你沟通。他们可能想,也可能不想把事情说一遍。你要足够了解他们,知道该怎么做。给他们食物,帮他们整理,给他们机会到你的艇上休息。在专注于下一次起航前,适时让他们进行热身。

Going Ashore 回岸

After the last race of the day, cruise up to each sailor in turn, and praise / encourage as merited. Give them something to eat and drink, and tow them in if the wind is light. Don't try or encourage discussion of the day's racing until later, to enable the competitors to come to terms with their results and look at their performance objectively. Ask parents to respect this rule; ideally the parents should not discuss the race with the competitor until after the debrief. The boats must be checked and packed away and the sailors changed, showered and fed.

在当天最后一场比赛结束后,依次驶向每一名水手,给予适当的赞扬/鼓励。提供食物和饮料,如果风小,就把他们拖回岸。先不要尝试或鼓励他们讨论当天的比赛,等选手们接受自己的比赛成绩,并能客观地看待自己的表现时,再进行沟通。让家长们也遵守这一原则;理想情况下,家长们在总结前不应与选手们讨论比赛。最后,检查船只并收船,洗澡,换衣服,吃饭。

Protests 抗议

Before heading home, the coach should wait for the end of 'Protest Time', to check for protests against the team or alterations to the sailing instructions for the next day.

在回家前,教练应一直等到"抗议时间"

结束，检查与团队相关的抗议或第二天航行细则的变更。

Protests are daunting for a young competitor at his first international event. Help by getting the protest form and rule book, and calmly talk over the incident. Guide the sailor to the most effective form of presentation of the case, both on paper and before the committee. Just by being present during the wait for the hearing, you will be a comfort and help to your team member.

初次参加国际赛事的年轻选手面对抗议时，可能会感到害怕。教练可以帮助他们获取抗议表格和规则手册，冷静地和他们讨论整个事件。引导选手以最有效的形式进行书面描述和在委员会面前陈述案件。你只要能够在选手等待听证的时候在场，就已经是对他们的安慰和帮助了。

The protest committee should allow you as a coach to go in the protest as an observer. This can be very helpful in debriefing the sailor on how they did in a protest and understanding the outcome of the protest. Do check with the sailor that it is ok to observe: this can make some sailors more nervous, but encourage them since it is so beneficial.

抗议委员会应该会允许你作为教练，出席抗议，进行旁听。这会非常有帮助，不仅方便你理解抗议结果，而且能更好地评价选手在抗议中的表现。当然，在参与前务必和选手确认他是否介意你进行旁观：有些水手可能会因此更加紧张，但要鼓励他们，因为这大有益处。

Check for protests
检查抗议

Debrief 总结

Hold the debrief for the day's racing at a pre-arranged time. Each race should be carefully analysed, and race-winning points noted. The coach should be available to speak to each competitor in turn privately. This gives the chance to go over any negative feelings. Hopefully perspectives will change, and a more positive attitude will be achieved.

在预先规划好的时间进行当天比赛的总结。应仔细分析每场比赛，记录好比赛获胜点。教练应轮流与每个选手私下交谈。这是帮助选手们克服负面情绪的好机会。他们的看法很可能会因此改变，变得更加积极。

Parents with experience and insight may contribute to the debrief, but you must be aware of possible inhibiting or attitude-modifying effects they will have on their offspring. This can be assessed in the pre-regatta training period; if in doubt about any parent, all should be excluded from the debrief.

一些有经验和洞察力的父母可能会在总结时提出很好的意见，但你必须意识到他们对自己的孩子可能产生的抑制，或对他们态度的影响。可在赛前培训期间进行评估；如果对父母的参与有疑虑，就不考虑让他们参与总结。

Hold a debrief after racing
赛后总结

Coaching Equipment
教学装备

The coach boat must be easily manoeuvrable with light steering and smooth throttle control. It is useful if the throttle control is on the left-hand side to make it easier to video for right handed coaches. A rigid-bottom inflatable-type boat is most suitable at sea, although cases can be made for other boat types in particular circumstances—for instance a Zodiac-type soft-bottom inflatable is seaworthy, versatile and easy to carry when deflated.

教练艇应易于操作，转向轻便且挡位控制流畅。如果挡位控制手柄位于左侧会很方便，对于右撇子教练来说，录视频会更容易些。硬底充气船最适合在海上使用，尽管在特定情况下也可能是其他船型，例如，Zodiac软底充气船，适用于航海、用途广泛且在放气后便于携带。

Your boat must have ground tackle that will hold in all conditions—at sea an anchor of adequate size with at least 4 m of chain and plenty of warp. It should also carry a waterproof tool kit with a plug spanner, a spare set of plugs, a spare prop and cotter pins, an emergency starting rope, an emergency fuel can and a tow line.

船上必须配备抛锚装备，以确保船在任何条件下都能抓地——足够大的海锚，配有至少4 m的链条和足够的锚绳。还应携带一个防水工具包，配有火花塞扳手、一套备用火花塞、备用螺旋桨和开口销、应急启动绳、应急燃料罐和拖船绳。

Other equipment you need:
所需的其他装备：
- **Race marks:** You will need at least two buoys, with anchors and warps. Small Dahn buoys with flags are practical.
- **竞赛浮标：** 至少需要两个浮标，且配有锚和锚绳。带有小旗子的小型带孔浮标非常实用。
- **Sound signal:** Cheapest and easiest is a whistle. Make sure it is loud enough. A good referee's whistle is recommended.
- **声音信号：** 口哨，最便宜最简单。确保吹起来声音足够大。建议配备一个好的裁判哨。
- **Sail battens:** Use them to signal start sequences.
- **帆骨：** 用于发出起航信号。
- **Hand-bearing compass / flag:** Use for windshift tracking.
- **手持指南针/旗帜：** 用于检查风摆。
- **Watertight box:** Use to carry a selection of the following according to coaching circumstances: VHF hand-held radio; clipboard and paper, pens and pencils; knife, pliers, screwdriver, small adjustable spanner; plastic tape, sailpalm, needle and thread; adhesive sail repair tape and scissors; shackles, sail ties, length of light low-stretch line; rule book; sunglasses, sunscreen; wind gauge; binoculars.
- **防水盒：** 根据教学情况，可选择携带以下物品：手持式甚高频对讲机、文件夹板和纸、钢笔和铅笔；刀、钳子、螺丝刀、小型活动扳手；胶带、补帆顶针、针和线；船帆修补胶带和剪刀；快挂、绑帆绳、一段轻的低弹性绳；规则书；太阳镜、防晒霜、风速仪；望远镜。
- **Tide stick:** To gauge the flow of the tide (can be used in conjunction with hand-held GPS).
- **潮汐棒：** 测量潮汐流速（可与手持GPS配合使用）。
- **Video camera** or a waterproof phone for videoing.
- **摄像机**或防水手机，用于录像。
- **For major events:** Spare foils, mast, sprit, ropes; food and drink for the troops; a large team or national flag.
- **重大赛事：** 备用舵和稳向板、桅杆、斜撑杆、绳子；团队的食物和饮料；一面大队旗或国旗。

Video Afloat
水上录像

Video can be used to demonstrate good technique and tactics; as an aid to tuning; and visualisation and mental rehearsal.

视频可用于向学员说明一些好的技巧和战术；辅助技术调整以及进行想象和心理排练。

However, there are some negatives which need to be borne in mind:

但是，视频的一些负面影响也要牢记：

CHAPTER 15 第十五章　　The Perfect Coach 完美教练

- It can be boring for sailors to watch lots of it—be selective
- 对于水手来说，观看大量视频可能会很无聊——视频要有选择性
- Taking pictures from a small boat in anything but calm weather can make you feel sick and can be difficult to watch
- 除了风平浪静的时候，任何天气在小船上拍摄，都可能导致晕船，而且内容也会模糊不清
- When used to demonstrate errors, it can lead to the competitor concerned suffering a loss of self-confidence
- 使用视频说明错误操作时，可能会导致当事人失去自信

When videoing, try to get close to the action, avoid using zoom
在拍摄视频时，尽量近景拍摄，避免使用放大功能

It is best for the coach to take their own video. They know what they want to show the sailors and what is important. Also, the coach can get very good at keeping the camera steady and they are normally driving the RIB, which is often the most stable part of the boat.

教练最好是自己拍摄，因为他们更清楚自己想向学员们说明什么以及重点是什么。而且教练更便于保持相机的稳定性，因为通常由他们来开艇，驾驶位一般是最稳的。

Great care needs to be taken while videoing and driving one-handed. Keep an eye on where you are going and what is happening around you, not just the video camera. With practice, this becomes easier.

在单手驾驶，拍摄视频时应格外小心。注意驾驶方向和周围的状况，不要只关注摄像。在反复练习后，水上拍摄会变得越来越容易。

Shooting Tips 拍摄技巧

- Try to keep the horizon at the same position in the frame
- 尽量保持地平线在画面中的同一位置
- Beware of using full zoom—it will magnify the camera's movement
- 注意不要使用完全放大功能——会放大相机的移动
- Never shoot into the sun except for artistic effect
- 不要对着太阳拍摄，除了追求艺术效果外
- Shooting angles should be either at right angles to the direction of movement or from ahead / astern
- 拍摄角度应与船的移动方向成直角，或从船头 / 船尾拍摄
- Ensure you are close enough to the boat to be able to see any important points
- 距离拍摄船只应足够近，以便拍到重点

At events it is often difficult to get close enough to get really good video, but it can often be used to show tactical and strategic situations. Consider taking pictures that can be blown up if you are too far away to video.

虽然在比赛中，通常很难靠得足够近，拍到特别好的视频，但是，一般都能用来说明战术和策略场景。如果你因离船太远无法录像，可考虑拍照，之后放大使用。

Replay 回放

Know what point you are trying to make when you show the video. First time show the video without comments. Second time make comments that are positive, constructive and not pointed.

明确你在播放视频时要表达的观点。第一次播放不加评论。第二次播放，给予正面的、有建设性的和温和的评论。

147

OPTIMIST RACING OP级帆船竞赛

Invite sailors to comment on their own tactics. Invariably they will know what they should have done, and don't need anybody else to point it out to them! Don't show videos that don't illustrate anything of use to the sailor.

邀请水手们评价自己的战术。他们肯定知道自己应该要做什么，不需要其他人指出来！不要给大家播放毫无用处的视频。

们绕上风标的名次是个好方法，如下所示：

Sailor 水手	1st Wdwd 第一次 绕上风标	2nd Wdwd 第二次 绕上风标	3rd Wdwd 第三次 绕上风标	Finish 结束
Becky	10	12	11	12
Jim	40	30	36	37

Target Chart 目标图

A target chart is useful as a means of evaluating a sailor's perceived ability and self-confidence. It is handy as a starting point for discussing training aims. Each sector concerns a particular skill. Sailors assess their ability in that skill on a score of 1–10 and shade in the sector accordingly.

目标图是评估水手感知能力和自信心的一种有效手段。作为初始水平，用于讨论培训目标非常方便。每个区域代表一项技能。水手们以1~10的分数评估自己某一技能的能力，然后相应地在该区域涂上阴影。

Use videos to illustrate points
使用视频说明要点

Monitoring Race Progress
跟踪比赛进展

Both in training and in a major event it is useful to record positions at every opportunity. This helps you to keep in touch with each individual's progress. It is easy to watch those that are doing well but lose touch with what is happening to the others. Later you will find it very handy to be able to show a disappointed sailor that they did at least do a brilliant second beat. A good method is to record windward mark placings for various promising sailors is like this:

无论是在训练，还是在重大赛事中，应抓住一切机会记录学员的名次。这有助于你了解每个人的进展。当然，我们很容易去关注那些做得好的学员，而忽略了其他人。而且，之后你还会发现，运用视频来鼓励灰心丧气的学员非常好用，可以很容易就向他们说明——至少他们在第二个迎风段表现非常出色。记录学员

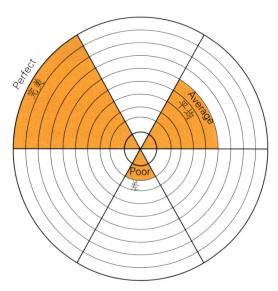

How to fill out a target chart
如何填充目标图

Target chart 目标图

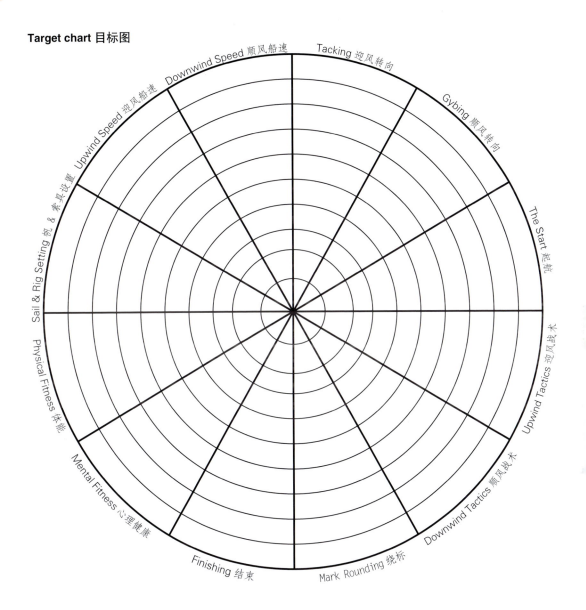

You can rate yourself on this target chart on the topics we have covered in this book.
你可以根据我们在本书中涵盖的主题，在目标图上给自己评分。

You can also use Training Record Sheets and Race Training Analysis Sheets (see next two pages).
你也可以使用培训记录表和竞赛培训分析表（请参阅后两页）。

These all can be downloaded from www.fernhurstbooks.com. Search for Optimist Racing and then click on 'Additional Resources'.
这些图表均可从网站 **www.fernhurstbooks.com** 下载，搜索《OP级帆船竞赛》（*Optimist Racing*），然后单击"其他资源"即可。

OPTIMIST RACING OP 级帆船竞赛

OPTIMIST TRAINING RECORD SHEET OP 培训记录表

Team 团队			Date 日期	
Venue 场地	Wind direction 风向		Wind Strength 风力	Sea state 海况
Sail 帆号	Mast Rake 桅杆倾度		Luff Tension 帆前缘张力	Outhaul 横拉器

Session & goals

Hours sailed:

Venue notes

Speed notes

What did you do & learn

Review—what do you need to do next

CHAPTER 15 第十五章　　The Perfect Coach 完美教练

RACE TRAINING ANALYSIS SHEET 竞赛培训分析表

Report No: 报告编号：	Event: 比赛：	Date: 日期：
Helm: 舵手：	Sail No: 帆号：	Boat Name: 船名：
Sail make: 帆厂：	Sail Cut: 帆形：	Sail Age: 船帆使用年限：

Wind Strength (steady? shifty? gusty?):
风力（稳定？风摆？阵风？）：

Sea State (smooth? choppy? swell?):
海况（平稳？起伏不定？波涛汹涌？）：

Waves (direction? effects? technique used?):
波浪（方向？影响？所用技术？）：

Luff Tension (number of twists on tack diagonal tie):
帆前缘张力（前帆角斜绑绳扭转次数）

Luff Shape (convex? straight? concave?):
帆前缘形态（凸起？平直？凹陷？）：

Top Tie Gap: 上端绑帆绳空隙：	Tack Tie Gap: 前帆角绑帆绳空隙：	Luff Tie Gap: 前帆缘绑帆绳空隙：

Outhaul Tension / Foot Shape:
横拉器张力/帆底形态：

Mast Rake:
桅杆倾度：

Daggerboard (vertical? forward? back? raised? how many cm?):
稳向板（垂直？往前？往后？抬起？多少cm？）：

Beat trim (upright? heeled to leeward? heeled to windward?):
迎风段调船（水平？倾向下风？倾向上风？）：

Balance (weather? lee? neutral helm?):
左右平衡（上风舵？下风舵？平衡舵？）：

Speed Upwind:
迎风船速：

Speed Downwind:
顺风船速：

Specific Problems:
具体问题：

Answers / Comments:
答案/评论：

Racing Notes 竞赛笔记

Pre-start: 起航前：	Start: 起航：
1st beat: 首个迎风航段：	Weather mark: 上风标：
Good points: 表现突出之处：	Problems: 问题：
Finish: 冲终点线：	Comments: 评论：

Copyright © 2019 Fernhurst Books Limited

Third edition published in 2019 by Fernhurst Books Limited

The Windmill, Mill Lane, Harbury, Leamington Spa, Warwickshire. CV33 9HP, UK
Tel: +44 (0) 1926 337488 | www.fernhurstbooks.com

First edition (by Phil Slater) published in 1995 by Fernhurst Books
Second edition (by Phil Slater) published 2001 by Fernhurst Books

All rights reserved. No part of this publication may be reproduced, stored in a retrieval system or transmitted, in any form or by any means, electronic, mechanical, photocopying, recording, scanning or otherwise, except under the terms of the Copyright, Designs and Patents Act 1988 or under the terms of a licence issued by The Copyright Licensing Agency Ltd, Saffron House, 6–10 Kirby Street, London EC1N 8TS, UK, without the permission in writing of the Publisher.

Designations used by companies to distinguish their products are often claimed as trademarks. All brand names and product names used in this book are trade names, service marks, trademarks or registered trademarks of their respective owners. The Publisher is not associated with any product or vendor mentioned in this book.

This publication is designed to provide accurate and authoritative information in regard to the subject matter covered. It is sold on the understanding that the Publisher is not engaged in rendering professional services. If professional advice or other expert assistance is required, the services of a competent professional should be sought. The Publisher accepts no responsibility for any errors or omissions, or for any accidents or mishaps which may arise from the use of this publication.

A catalogue record for this book is available from the British Library ISBN 978-1-912177-18-9

The authors and publisher would like to express their considerable thanks to:
The Turkish Optimist sailors (Okyanus Arikan, Mert Aydoğan, MustafacanÖztuncel, Kuzey Kumlali, BulutÇanakçi), the Turkish Sailing Federation and photographer Sedat Yilmaz for the photos from Turkey © Sedat Yilmaz.
Derin Can and Dilara Soyer and their parents Anette and Orkun for the photos at Draycote Water Sailing Club by Jeremy Atkins © Fernhurst Books.

Milo Gill-Taylor for the photos at Spinnaker Sailing Club by Tim Hore © Fernhurst Books.

Front cover photograph © Mark Yuill / shutterstock.com
Back cover photograph © Sedat Yilmaz
Other photographs by:
Tom Gruitt: p9; Steve Irish: p20, 74, 87; Optimax: p71; Jeremy Atkins: p45, 62, 63, 84
Designed & illustrated by Daniel Stephen
Printed in the UK by Latimer Trend

Taking a fresh look at the complex subject of racing to get you moving up the leaderboard

View our entire list at www.fernhurstbooks.com

Sign up to receive details of new books & exclusive special offers at
www.fernhurstbooks.com/register

Get to know us more on **social media**

FERNHURST|BOOKS

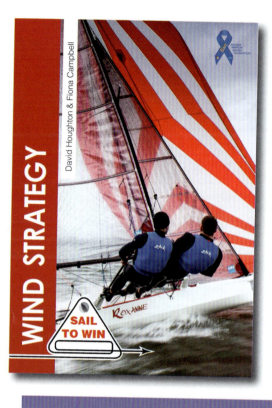

WIND STRATEGY

David Houghton & Fiona Campbell

SAIL TO WIN

CHAPTER 5
Wind Facts: Gusts & Lulls

The wind varies on every timescale, from seconds to minutes to hours to days and even longer. It is the short period variations in the order of minutes which are normally described as gusts and lulls.

Gusts & Lulls Due To Thermal Overturning
We saw in Chapter 2 that many gusts and lulls are a result of air overturning near the sea or land surface when the air aloft, which has not been slowed or backed by friction at the surface, comes down to replace what has been subject to friction. A common cause of this overturning is thermal; when air warmed at the surface becomes buoyant, rises, and is replaced by air from aloft. This is the most easy to understand.

On many days, particularly when there is a regular pattern of cumulus clouds, the gusts and lulls arrive at fairly regular intervals. In these conditions the normal surface wind is blowing in the normal way and super-imposed on it is an overturning motion, upwards underneath the cumulus clouds and downwards between them (below). The descending air has not experienced friction near the surface so it has approximately the horizontal speed and direction of the gradient wind. It is significantly veered and stronger than the wind which has spent some time near the surface. In other words it is a gust. The air under each cloud has spent time near the surface, has been slowed and backed by friction – it is a lull. Thermally driven gusts and lulls have one clearly defined characteristic: a gust is always veered and stronger in contrast with a lull, which is always backed and lighter.

Timescale & Size Of Shift
If the cumulus clouds are small and relatively close together they indicate a relatively short time between gusts and lulls – perhaps 3 minutes or so. The swing in wind is typically in the order of 5 to 10 degrees in direction and 5 to 10 per cent in speed. If the clouds are larger and further apart a longer time interval is indicated – perhaps 10 to 15 minutes – and the shifts may be less regular and larger. If the convection becomes so deep that the cumulus clouds turn into cumulonimbus and showers develop, completely different wind characteristics are experienced. They are described in Chapter 15.

The clouds causing gusts & lulls

WIND STRATEGY

Gradient Wind Blowing Along Line Of Valley
The surface wind will blow approximately in the same direction as the gradient, but its strength will depend on the stability of the air in the valley, and whether the valley is closed or open. If the valley provides a clear route through a mountain range the wind will funnel strongly along it, particularly when the air is stable and therefore reluctant to rise over the mountains (below).

Open valley funnelling the wind

Gradient Wind Blowing Across Valley
The air flow is likely to separate, and the steeper the slope the more readily it separates. The eddy forms on the side of the valley towards the gradient wind. The steeper the side the larger the eddy (A is larger than B in the diagram below).

Gradient wind blowing across the valley creates an eddy - the steeper the slope, the longer the eddy

Peninsulas
Let's look first at a relatively small peninsula, the size of Cornwall or Auckland, for instance. In the absence of a gradient wind, on a sunny day a sea breeze develops onto all shores (below), but the breezes onto the opposite major shores dominate and progress inland until they meet in the middle of the peninsula where a line of cumulus clouds may be seen. Once the two breezes meet they die. Then after 10 to 20 minutes or so the land warms again and the sea breeze process starts all over. To sustain sea breezes onto both shores throughout the afternoon without faltering the peninsula must be in the order of 100 km wide.

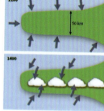

Sea breeze cycle on a 50 km peninsular

In the diagram top right, the direction of the gradient wind is along the line of the peninsula. The most significant feature is the bands of stronger and lighter winds respectively to be found just offshore. It is important to note that it will take only a small swing in wind direction to support a sea breeze onto one of the major shores. Starting from a wind parallel to the line of the peninsula, a shift of only 5 degrees may tip the balance in favour of a sea breeze onto one or other shore, a shift probably outside the accuracy of the forecast. The onus is on you, the sailor on the spot, to interpret the wind trends observed on the water.

The middle diagram is a case for a good Quadrant 1 sea breeze onto the downwind shore, but a peninsula width of over 70 km is probably necessary for its full strength potential to be reached. Sea breezes generally penetrate inland at a speed of between 10 and 20 km per hour. From your knowledge of the width of the peninsula you can make a very rough estimate of how long it will be before it gets to the other shore and starts to die.

The peninsula situation in the bottom diagram is interesting. The breeze starts onto the end at B, a Quadrant 1 situation, but as it veers and backs to the coastline it increases on the more southerly-facing coast, and dies away at B with some bending of the wind around the corner.

Spain
Spain is a good example of a very large peninsula, and winds around Spain in the summer are a good example of a Quadrant 3 situation. For much of the summer the weather map shows a shallow low pressure area over the country, and each day the pressure falls some 3 to 5 millibars due to the heating of the land, recovering at night. The detailed shape of the isobars varies from day to day. It is often influenced by thunderstorms breaking out in late afternoon and continuing into the night, especially in late summer. On average the morning gradient wind is parallel to the coast and just in Quadrant 3, light southerly on the Mediterranean coast, light northerly on the Atlantic coast, and so on. Every afternoon the thermal vector, also parallel to the coast, enhances the morning wind to give an afternoon onshore wind typically in the range of Force 2 to 4 at an angle of about 15 to 20 degrees to the coast. It is blowing onshore but is not a sea breeze, and does not have the important characteristic of a sea breeze, which is to be strongest close to the coast.

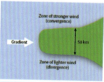

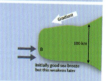

The effect of the gradient wind on different sized peninsulas

TRAINING TO WIN

Jon Emmett

SAIL TO WIN

TRAINING TO WIN

Stepping Stone Upwind
▲▲▲▲

Sail to the windward mark, and round correctly, sail downwind for 2 boat lengths with sail controls etc. fully adjusted for the downwind and then stop. Then use a Rabbit Start to start again upwind to a new windward mark which you round, sail downwind for 2 boat lengths and then stop. And then repeat with another Rabbit Start and upwind leg to a new windward mark, and so on.

This exercise could also be used as a way of progressing to the intended race area rather than towing, or an extended warm-up for getting to a race area, or a way of taking people back to shore and keeping them focused.

Depending upon the venue, it may be extremely important to train on the precise race area to experience the same currents, waves, wind, etc.

Keelboat-Style Steering
▲▲▲▲

Going fast in any boat is about steering the optimum angle to the next mark and so this is a good exercise to focus on steering, separate from the other elements of hiking / trapezing and trimming we discussed earlier. It is all too easy to steer too much or just use all your bodyweight to 'bully' the boat around the course, especially if you are young and fit. So, in this exercise, you sit 'keelboat-style': sitting on the side deck but in reverse, with your legs pointing out (be careful not to drag your feet in the water as it will slow you down). This means that your body weight is fixed and it may even be hard to sheet. This makes good steering suddenly the main focus of your attention.

Sailing keelboat-style

This exercise can be easy or difficult:

Easy	Free sailing keelboat style
Medium	Sail around a course keelboat style
Hard	Racing keelboat style

50

TRAINING TO WIN

Advanced Techniques

Holding A Lane

Very often after a start you must hold your lane (continuing on your existing tack at good VMG without being affected by the boats around you through dirty air / leebow effect etc.) because otherwise you will get bad air or have to sail a lot of extra distance:
- If you try to go low, then you may end up being leebowed by the boat to leeward
- If you try to pinch, someone to windward is likely to roll you and give you dirty air as well
- If you tack you may have to duck many boats and sail a greater distance

In these scenarios it is best to keep going (as fast as you can!) until an opportunity presents itself to do something different.

So, being able to hold your lane is very important. The higher the level of competition the more important this becomes.

Often you may have to hold your lane with other boats in very close proximity, either because you definitely want to go one way (for example, if there is an expected shift or there is better current) or because you are not in a position to tack without having to duck a lot of boats and thereby lose a lot of places.

Lane Hold
▲▲▲

The perfect exercise for this is the Lane Hold: there is a standard 3,2,1, go sequence, but the aim is to get upwind on one tack to level with a buoy, perhaps a 3-minute sail upwind.

Of course, in a real race, after a poor start a boat may be able to get out of the dirty air / leebow effect by footing off (losing some ground to windward but better than sailing in dirty air) or tacking off (again getting into clear air). But the point of this exercise is to learn when you can hold a clear lane and when you can't. The narrower the lane you can hold the better, so pushing it to the limit in training will help you understand this.

After the start, try to hold your lane for 3 minutes

Rabbit Start

It is not always possible to have starting marks or, indeed, someone to monitor the line. A Rabbit Start is a great way of starting an exercise and it also practises your ability to judge speed and distance.

Rabbit Start
▲▲▲

The 'Rabbit' sails across the fleet on a close-hauled course (very important they don't reach in at speed as everyone has to be able to judge their approach). Boats then cross at full speed, on a close-hauled course behind the Rabbit.

When everyone has passed behind the Rabbit, the Rabbit tacks (maybe 2 boats past the last boat, but this is wind strength and boat class dependent).

Rabbit Start

Controlling The Boat

The most important thing is controlling the boat. The advanced exercises overleaf will really push some of you to practise on your own, others in groups. These are time and distance / boat handling exercises. Remember that, even though you will typically be lining up on starboard tack on a start line, you should also practise on port tack because these are incredibly useful boat handling exercises in their own right.

There are individual exercises and group exercises shown overleaf.

CHAPTER 2 Starting

THE ANDREW SIMPSON SAILING FOUNDATION

The charity was founded to honour the life and legacy of Andrew 'Bart' Simpson MBE, Olympic Gold & Silver medalist and America's Cup Sailor by using sailing to improve the lives of young people.

Working with sailing providers internationally, the Foundation offers the challenges of a sailing environment to promote health and wellbeing, and to develop personal skills that will improve a young person's ability to succeed in life.

SUPPORT US

info@andrewsimpsonsailing.org
andrewsimpsonfoundation.org

- @AndrewSimpsonSa
- Andrew Simpson Sailing Foundation
- andrewsimpsonsailingfoundation
- sailonbart